Soul Keeping Company

LUCIE BROCK-BROIDO is the author of three collections of poetry, *A Hunger*, *The Master Letters* and *Trouble in Mind* (all published by Alfred A. Knopf, New York). In 2008 she published *Letters to a Stranger: The Collected Poems of Thomas James* with Graywolf Press in the US. She is Director of Poetry in the School of the Arts at Columbia University and has taught previously at Harvard University, the Bennington Writing Seminars and Princeton University. She has been the recipient of awards from the John Simon Guggenheim Foundation, the National Endowment for the Arts and the American Academy of Arts and Letters. She lives in New York City and in Cambridge, Massachusetts.

Also available from Carcanet Press

Five American Poets: An Anthology (Robert Hass, John Matthias, James McMichael, John Peck, Robert Pinsky)

John Ashbery
Self-Portrait in a Convex Mirror
A Worldly Country
Notes from the Air: Selected Later Poems
Planisphere

Louise Glück
The Wild Iris
Averno
A Village Life

Jorie Graham
The Dream of the Unified Field: Selected Poems
Overlord
Sea Change

Marilyn Hacker
Essays on Departure: New and Selected Poems 1980–2005

Edward Hirsch
The Living Fire: New and Selected Poems 1975–2010

Richard Howard
Inner Voices: Selected Poems 1963-2003

Brigit Pegeen Kelly
Poems: Song and The Orchard

Robert Rehder
First Things When

Stephen Rodefer
Call It Thought: Selected Poems

LUCIE BROCK-BROIDO

Soul Keeping Company

Selected Poems

CARCANET

First published in Great Britain in 2010 by
Carcanet Press Limited
Alliance House
Cross Street
Manchester M2 7AQ

A Hunger Copyright © 1988 by Lucie Brock-Broido
The Master Letters Copyright © 1995 by Lucie Brock-Broido
Trouble in Mind Copyright © 2004 by Lucie Brock-Broido
Published by arrangement with Alfred A. Knopf, a division of Random House, Inc.

Selection copyright © Lucie Brock-Broido 2010
Indexes copyright © Grant Shipcott 2010

The right of Lucie Brock-Broido to be identified as the author of this work
has been asserted by her in accordance with the
Copyright, Designs and Patents Act of 1988
All rights reserved

A CIP catalogue record for this book is available from the British Library

ISBN 978 1 85754 840 2

The publisher acknowledges financial assistance from Arts Council England

Typeset by XL Publishing Services, Tiverton
Printed and bound in England by SRP Ltd, Exeter

Contents

from *A Hunger* (1988)

Domestic Mysticism	3
Birdie Africa	5
Evolution	8
Real Life	9
Autobiography	10
October Seventh, Nineteen Eighty-Three	11
The Future as a Cow	13
Edward VI on the Seventh Day	14
Jessica, from the Well	17
Hitchcock Blue	22
Kid Flash	23
Heartbeat	25
Danse Macabre	26
What the Whales Sound Like in Manhattan	27
The Beginning of the Beginning	28
In a Landlocked Time	29
Lucie & Her Sisters	31
Elective Mutes	33
I Wish You Love	38
Ten Years Apprenticeship in Fantasy	40
And So Long, I've Had You Fame	42
After the Grand Perhaps	43

from *The Master Letters* (1995)

A Preamble to *The Master Letters*	49
Carrowmore	51
Also, None Among Us Has Seen God	52
Rome Beauty	53
Unholy	54
A Brief History of Asylum	55
The Supernatural Is Only the Natural, Disclosed	57

Obsession, Compulsion	58
Carnivorous	59
To a Strange Fashion of Forsaking	60
Did Not Come Back	61
And You Know That I Know Milord That You Know	62
The October Horse	63
Gratitude	65
Dull Weather	66
From the Proscenium	67
Radiating Naïveté	69
Fair Copy from a Fair World	71
His Apprentice	72
You Can't Always Get What You Want	73
Pursuit of Happiness	74
A Glooming Peace This Morning with It Brings	75
Housekeeping	76
Haute Couture Vulgarity	77
Toxic Gumbo	79
In the Attitude Desired for Exhibition	80
Like Murder for Small Hay in the Underworld	81
Everybody Has a Heart, Except Some People	82
Moving On in the Dark Like Loaded Boats at Night, Though There Is No Course, There Is Boundlessness	83
Your Cromwell, Your Thomas More	84
I Dont Know Who It Is, That Sings, nor Did I, Would I Tell	85
Grimoire	86
Work	87
The Last Passenger Pigeon in the Cincinnati Zoo	89
Everything Husk to the Will	90
The Interrupted Life	93
How Can It Be I Am No Longer I	94
The Sleeping Hollow of His Face Will Be the Straight Pass of Surrendering	96
Am Moor	97

from *Trouble in Mind* (2004)

The Halo That Would Not Light	101
After Raphael	102
Leaflet on Wooing	103
Still Life with Aspirin	104
Herculaneum	106
The One Theme of Which Everything Else Is a Variation	107
Periodic Table of Ethereal Elements	108
Some Details of Hell	109
Basic Poem in a Basic Tongue	110
Death as a German Expert	111
Gamine	112
Morgue Near Heaven	113
The Insignificants	114
A Lion in Winter	115
Boy at the Border of His Own Allegory	116
Still Life with Feral Horse	117
Soul Keeping Company	118
Self-Portrait with Her Hair on Fire	119
The Deerhunting	120
Darwinism as Spite	121
Lady with an Ermine	122
Fragment on Dissembling	122
The Halo That Lit Twice	123
Self-Portrait as Kaspar Hauser	124
Self-Portrait with Self-Pity	125
Girl at the Border of Her Own Allegory	126
Of the Finished World	127
In Elsinore	128
Spain	129
Portrait of Lucy with Fine Nile Jar	130
The Identity of the Bridegroom	132
Self-Portrait as a Herd of One	133
Physicism	134
Self-Portrait with Her Hair Cut Off	135
The One Thousand Days	136
Dire Wolf	138

Pamphlet on Ravening	139
Self-Deliverance by Lion	140
Notes on the Poems	143
Index of Titles	155
Index of First Lines	158

from
A HUNGER
(1988)

*For my father
Joel Greenwald
with love*

Domestic Mysticism

In thrice 10,000 seasons, I will come back to this world
In a white cotton dress. Kingdom of After My Own Heart.
Kingdom of Fragile. Kingdom of Dwarves. When I come home,
Teacups will quiver in their Dresden saucers, pentatonic chimes
Will move in wind. A covey of alley cats will swarm on the side
Porch & perch there, portents with quickened heartbeats
You will feel against your ankles as you pass through.

After the first millennium, we were supposed to die out.
You had your face pressed up against the coarse dyed velvet
Of the curtain, always looking out for your own transmigration:
What colors you would wear, what cut of jewel,
What kind of pageantry, if your legs would be tied
Down, if there would be wandering tribes of minstrels
Following with woodwinds in your wake.

This work of mine, the kind of work which takes no arms to do,
Is least noble of all. It's peopled by Wizards, the Forlorn,
The Awkward, the Blinkers, the Spoon-Fingered, Agnostic Lispers,
Stutterers of Prayer, the Flatulent, the Closet Weepers,
The Charlatans. I am one of those. In January, the month the owls
Nest in, I am a witness & a small thing altogether. The Kingdom
Of Ingratitude. Kingdom of Lies. Kingdom of *How Dare I*.

I go on dropping words like little pink fish eggs, unawares, slightly
Illiterate, often on the mark. Waiting for the clear whoosh
Of fluid to descend & cover them. A train like a silver
Russian love pill for the sick at heart passes by
My bedroom window in the night at the speed of mirage.
In the next millennium, I will be middle aged. I do not do well
In the marrow of things. Kingdom of Trick. Kingdom of Drug.

In a lung-shaped suburb of Virginia, my sister will be childless
Inside the ice storm, forcing the narcissus. We will send
Each other valentines. The radio blowing out
Vaughan Williams on the highway's purple moor.
At nine o'clock, we will put away our sewing to speak
Of lofty things while, in the pantry, little plants will nudge
Their frail tips toward the light we made last century.

When I come home, the dwarves will be long
In their shadows & promiscuous. The alley cats will sneak
Inside, curl about the legs of furniture, close the skins
Inside their eyelids, sleep. Orchids will be intercrossed & sturdy.
The sun will go down as I sit, thin armed, small breasted
In my cotton dress, poked with eyelet stitches, a little lace,
In the queer light left when a room snuffs out.

I draw a bath, enter the water as a god enters water:
Fertile, knowing, kind, surrounded by glass objects
Which could break easily if mishandled or ill-touched.
Everyone knows an unworshipped woman will betray you.
There is always that promise, I like that. Kingdom of Kinesis.
Kingdom of Benevolent. I will betray as a god betrays,
With tenderheartedness. I've got this mystic streak in me.

Birdie Africa

for Stanley Kunitz

Wolf

My father calls me Wolf.
He says that I will see things other people will not see
at night. When he holds me, heat comes out
of his big arms & I belong to him.
In the cold of Christmastime he rocks
me in his deep lap in the great shadow of a comforter.
We are wool on wool,
back & forth, singing these songs
whose words I can't even say out loud.
I think they're about God who keeps us in his paws.
My mother watches, standing at my window, arms
folded to her chest. One fingerbone
of moonlight reaches in, tapping on the lock
of her face, restless, not like a mother wolf
but lit like she is going
somewhere else.
But when I wind my arms around
him, put my face into the dimmed scoop
of his neck, he smells like good warm fire
like dark sweet dreams.

The Roof

I sleep on the roof now.
She has taken me away from him.
I sleep thinking of his face tucked
next to mine like a big black bear.
There are other children now.
We run like wild

animals. We let our hair go
into puzzles which will never be unraveled.
We let our teeth go fierce.
We leave dirt in our palms
& sleep without nightclothes.
We pee in the yards & eat raw things.
In the dark we watch the traffic lights blinking
from our sleep in the cold night air.
Sometimes I talk to the stars
& the stars keep the traffic
in the sky from bottling up.
Each person gives off a little
torch when they sleep
& mine's the softest one.

Birdie

I am Birdie now I don't know why.
I squat at the edge of the top
of our rowhouse & I'm without wings I think.
Philadelphia isn't gentle now. Bad things echo up
& down our neighborhood at night.
I think we wound the people of our street.
I am hurting myself.
I can't tell time you know.

All the Africas

All the Africas live here
like a family of fire.
My mother always wears the bone of moon
across her face. I peer at her
like through a keyhole & I don't know why.
She never touches me.
The grownups eat cooked things

& we go foraging,
carving our designs in trees
& benches in the park & cedar picnic tables
left out in the trash, we never leave our names
& we can't read.
I am the clean seed
of a new race springing
from the dark continent of America.
God keeps me pure & savage here
before Moses
before the gift
before TV & toothbrushes
before the alphabet.

The Last Africa

The man with the megaphone warns Vincent Leaphart
to get out. He stays on, we stay here with him.
From up top of the bunker, the city
is our karroo dotted with colors of light.
In the dark, we are swept
down to the belly of our house.
They turn water on us
like a devil. We stay on.
We are flooding, there is no light left.
Then the fires & we huddle in the basement
under wet green blankets. Everything smells bad.
My mother stops twisting & I don't know why.
Everybody wailing. I am Birdie & I don't know how.
Then a quiet like I've never heard before.
Ramona Africa pulls me outside to the alley
& I burn there with her, naked on the stones
in the sweet jungle of the city.
When I come home my father will be singing
like an old kind dream. I have seen things
at night that other people have not seen.

Evolution

The extinct creatures would have liked this day,
a festival flooded all the way to the river.

If they were still alive with us, they would curl
into the leaves left from last autumn,
begin their long journey to be coal.
Someday, they would be precious minerals.

They might have been confused,
the cello playing solo,
these brief black strokes
the Chinese character for rain.

But they would have understood
the love of old leaves heaped,
the dogs barking down
the late afternoons, howling for summertime.

What I want is to sleep away an epoch,
wake up as a girl with another kind of heart.

In the Vatican library, the letters
to Anne Boleyn are pinned down to keep
from coiling. An entire country
changed its faith once for its king.

I want to know what the letters say & go on
saying, what her face looked like in sleep.

By supper the invalids will be lying
down, whorled in white coverlets,
exhausted from yearning.
Everything they do is smaller than these
who walked in a world
that was greener than this one.

I am the medieval child in the basket, rocking.
Feigning sleep, up all night listening for secrets:
why there are punishments,
what news bad weather brings,
how things get winnowed out.

Real Life

Soon the electrical wires will grow heavy under the snow.
I am thinking of fire of the possibility of fire & then moving

Across America in a car with a powder blue dashboard,
Moving to country music & the heart

Is torn a little more because the song says the truth.
Because in the thirty-six things that can happen

To people, men & women, women & women,
Men & men, in all these things the soul is bound

To be broken somewhere along the line,
That clove-scented, air-colored wanderer blushing

With no memory, no inkling & then proceeds
Across America

In the sap green of the tropics,
Toward the cadmium of a bitter sunrise to a new age,

At the white impossible ice hour, starving,
Past the electric blue of the rivers melting down,

Above the nude, snuff, terra cotta, maybe fire,
Over the tiny fragile mound of finger bones

from A HUNGER

Of an Indian who died standing up,
Through the heliotrope of a song about the sunset,

To live the thirty-six things
& never comes home.

Autobiography

It is only three o'clock & already I'm alone
Listening to the lovers next door
Like Patsy Cline & her Man
Throwing barebacked wooden furniture
Like the real life bicker of true love.
I love that hands-on,
Die-while-you're-dark-haired-still
& young, fists curled to desire,
Take Me kind of love.
They'll make love without apology
& I'll be left to the afternoon
& the autoerotic sounds of my American voice
Getting it all down.

October Seventh, Nineteen Eighty-Three

When everything seems a message,
A small cue of light beneath the door,
Shadows that move too early
When the thing which they are mimicking
Is still, the car crash at Lochlyn
In the middle of the dawn
& no survivors anywhere in sight.

Not that I don't have the same chemicals
That everyone else has too.
It isn't that I am alone
Or that my certain breed
Of bliss catches fire in the wrong
Times & I'm bewildered with a joy
So large I could expire.

Tonight is my ten thousandth night.
It happens in the middle of my twenty-seventh
Year. I am one-third done with this.
It happens suddenly, without warning, like the loss
Of signal lanterns in electric storms,
Like a wound appearing out of nowhere
Where before there was clean flesh.

I kept hearing about the Underground
In reckless cities all over the world,
How important danger will become in a tunnel
Situation. How caution means nothing,
How the music of traveling too fast
Has everything to do with risk & melancholia.
I am drawn to figments & occasion:

from A HUNGER

REM sleep, Winter Solstice, the Blind Man's
Afternoons. I would read for him
In a Cambrian room which smelled of dread
& dance there for him barefoot
On a black rug, as if he could see
The color of the inside of my mouth
From a room six thousand miles away.

I have come to this. Those of us whose eyes
By chance, genetics, aptitude, go down
On the ends will be perceived as perpetually sad.
There is nothing quite exact to fear
& these are hours of exactitude.

As if it would be possible to live
In random increments or know
That no one knows which thing
Will happen next. This many days
Into my life, I have come to this.

October, I am in possession of my name.
Sorcerer, this is substantial life we're speaking of.
Light, you loom upon these days
As if everything has its certain purpose
Like an inebriated monk illuminating a great text.

The Future as a Cow

I can't say the future is not a cow.
The cow may be my future. I don't know.
                    MANUTE BOL

From the great warm side of the animal
heaving with meat, as she breathes out
the day tightens to this rare night.

The herds put their faces as close to the ground
as possible, listening for what grows
& moves, for what is kind, the stuff
of this dark earth, clean as the day
before this day, we were the only ones alive
preparing for the news of some momentous thing.

I like this world like no one
else has ever liked this world.
I can't say there isn't a certain
amount of radioactivity. I can't say
anyone will save anyone

because I know
by now about cherishing & miraculous deaths
& the deep days of summer which lie
ahead of us & I might know
what is lost

as the girls in North Dakota waken in the midst
of their own blonde hair & tie it back
with grosgrain, startled somewhere in the middle
of this landlocked dream, or that they had dreamt
of anything other than bliss,
one you can know, but never have.

That what is lost
cannot be gotten back.

from A HUNGER

& the animals move together
bunching,
grazing their softest parts
against the ground, each other,
most vulnerable of all.

I took care of the cows. I looked for animals
which would like to kill the cows.
Sometimes I talk out loud to keep them away.

Edward VI on the Seventh Day

I

Father is a large man
he has what I have not yet known
a passion, he has greatness in his gowns
& all of England at his beck & call.
I know when he is walking how I love
to hear the airs about him echo
in the halls are great & frigid as his foot
steps hard & harrowing come toward my room
& here I wait for him, he is superior.

II

His robes are deep with steam
& blue, he rarely touches me.
But listens by each morning from the door's
bold other wooden side, my voice is high
he listens as I sing my lessons louder
when I hear the footsteps stop
his breath is big, I want so much to please
him, then he bursts inside to see me

small blue boy, a version miniature
stand shortly on a velvet chair, recite
the Classics, beaming. But I never smile
near him, must not laugh.
I will be him someday.

III

I am, by far, too fair for him.
He is dark & brilliant with a temper, fire
I am airy, scampering. The ladies say
that I am frail, my fingers womanish.
He doesn't know me, know that I am quite
so small & elegant as this.
It is a son, October
when he bellowed & the corridors
went marbled with a blaze & heat
& it was I, small thing, that made him bellow
when my mother died it was: a son.
I will learn to move the air about me widely
as he does, an animal as wild & vile with scent
a face as terrible & bearded, hands
as loud & difficult as his, as passionate.

IV

A blue night in November when we stood
outside together with the owls & hounds
all bothered by the first chill evening howling
when our breath made muted billowings of talk
the things he told me made some ice upon his whiskers
& he is quite excitable when he is cold I think.
He told me what is power & he told me why
I must grow tall, he told me when to set the bells
in motion for a death or for the sake of bliss
he said, or for a hunger, for a woman.
He told me how to dance he told me everything.

from A HUNGER

V

The first time that I set the bells
in motion will be morning.
By the light of day, a season changing
one to two & tolling two to one
that much the smaller then to none.
White winter & in January I am him.

VI

& all of England at my beckoned call.

VII

Earth it is the last grey winter all consumed
the lack of angles & the smoothness watered
of a child's face. I was to be a man by now
& heralding the pierce green matters of the spring.
By evening I am thin & underripe
as pale as masks all meant for ghosts
& things of underground all spirited
& newborn in their vapoured states.
He told me then
he told me everything
I've never danced
& now these humours all confused:
black bile, blood & I am chilled the bells
are counting hours like the years of me
not happened yet, too many hours as the bells
are moving wind about them, hallowing & huge
& passing once then twice now past the midnight
I am fevered I am pretty
in a plague of white & bells
are calling out the days & seasons
in Westminster Abbey, vaulting
& the bells are coughing
I was of my father I am King.

Jessica, from the Well

I

This is what it was like: the morning
pale all above me, a patch of sky
like a blue poker flung into a floor
of earth, this is what I have to go on.
I am on my knees at first, a Jessica
a prayer—I pray against the rose
caliche, the hardpan rock, a marbling
of new wound in my forehead.
I've never spoken aloud yet to anyone
alive, but I know all the words.

On Wednesday morning I slipped down
the shaft like the small mythic creature
I have always known I ought to be.
No one was looking.
I am mutable still, I fold myself.
It is a gift to be this small & aboriginal.
Even without food, I am growing
& I find this frightful that my body
will become too large to live here comfortably.
The earth opens for me
as I always knew it would for a wish.

II

All day, I am divined
by sunlight & October has gone
damask, ocherous. When I learn a word
sometimes, I am compelled to use it.
Given my disposition, I will always be
circuitous, precocious, an Embellisher.
Like Oskar, I can make a world

change with my voice, can shatter the diamond
tipped bits of the drill, can make the wells' walls glitter
back at me. My own voice travels sideways
as it zigzags to the titian center
of the earth & curls back up to me
like a seamstress' needle against her thimble
in the very center of the Taj Mahal.
I am the only one alive.

By dusk, I am running out
of ways to warm myself.
I have warmed my self with my self.
My own limbs curled all about me, fetal.
Sometimes, I am so obvious like that.
I sing & somewhere above, they can hear me
humming along with myself & myself.
A choir of me's.
By nightfall, only a small albino fracture
will be left of the moon
& I will have lost all light to navigate.
Soon I will be famous.

III

By midnight, I can hear my own heart thump
against the well, dry for a million miles
till it hits the water corrugated by the beating
as it ripples back to me. It is instantly
recognizable, the way a mother cat knows
her own by scent & self love. It is me.
Before this day, my skin was never marred
& Quaker pink. My forehead has opened now
quite by happenstance, the etching on a wall
of an undiscovered cave, unlucky hieroglyph.

Take, for instance, my right leg
which, by midnight, I have accidentally wedged
in a notorious & irredeemable position.

I hate to be unnatural, especially in personal geometry
& by now, the leg has lodged irrevocably up
against my face, unbound, unfortunate.
There is to be no turning
back & I will sing & think of crying
for the first time so they'll know
at last I've blundered. I lean
into the rock, a willful child, a little bruised
& if I go out I will die dreaming.

IV

I had forgotten the small news of the night
between dreams & waking into the warm
smooth blown air shimmying down the oval
of the well. In the whole history of song
I know very few. So this is what it's like.
I am fixing on the hemp clothesline
strung across Aunt Jamie Moore's backyard,
on last week's laundered sheets, triangled
like sails, splashed with hyacinth & vetch
they stiffen in the wind against a Texan cobalt
sky. It is dawn. All night long
my eyes widened to accommodate the lack
of light, a self-illumined glowfish flat
on its side, I keep my flicker constant, wide awake
while sleeping, both eyes ajar.

Big gangly weepy gamey men, Sweethearts & Insomniacs,
keep prodding me   *to sing.*
And I sing.

And: *Move your foot for me, Juicy.*
And I wiggle it back for the man.

And: *How does a kitten go?*
And I go like a kitten goes, on

& on in that throaty liquid lewd bowlegged
voice like kittens make.
Then shut these big ole eyes.

V

Someday, I will be buried above ground
like Monroe, vaulted
always in the midst of flowers & sentiment.
On the descent, I was magically compact
boneless, as agile as water itself always
on the way toward other water.
The noise of my own form against the loosening
walls as I am born into the dark
rococo teratogenic rooms of the underground.
All the noise of the world
stops here & muffles, muffles me.
This town knows how to drill.
Sometimes my imagination gets to running wild.

Bring me back
alive. It was so simple to come down.
I wake with my own hair wound
into my fist, in sleep I've torn my own
self   —*pretty, milky curls.*
A spool of me.
In the matter of my toes, there has been damage done
but when I come back, they'll pinken up I'm sure.
In America: *Hard Work & Prayer.*
Resilience is bliss in the body,
the voodoo of immunity,
the will to come back,
Deliverance.

VI

Surrounded by jelly, an accoutrement of eros for ascent
from the well, I am born.
Wide eyed & swaddled in white linens, I emerge
pristine & preserved, like some Egyptian form
accompanied & gifted
with all the Nilotic charms
necessary for the long quicksilver moments
of the Afterlife.
So this is it.
I rub my eyes in newslight as if awakening
from the mere corn yellow husks
of slumber of an ordinary lateday nap.

The heart is left   *in situ*, I am lifted
from the oubliette
divine by water, blinking by air.
I cannot speak a word yet, but I know them all.
I sing, holding a piece of myself in my hand,
it is hair & fear & the church bells muscle
against each other
& the earth opens for me
as I always knew it would for a myth.
Given my character, I will always be mercurial,
a little sentimental, star-shaped & terrestrial
divine by water, healed by air
luminescent, inconceivable, a prayer
a Jessica,   *I sing.*

from A HUNGER

Hitchcock Blue

These we take for granted:
The blue turn of the water at Three.
The bones of the lover alone
Still life in Prussian blue.
The blonde in the fur cap
At the northern seaport in late November.
These given which we have come to regard:
Anima, Animus

I have gone into the fire & lived
There. I told you in a letter
You touch it only once, you watch it
For awhile you enter the flame.
The blue part of the scald, the part
That mars the skin, remembering
It will not forgive, forever.
That's a pretty thing.

We imagined life without that auburn heat
Of the south, ultra marine by day, direct.
Aniline & dangerous by dusk, midnight
Blue by midnight as we lay together in that blue
Of blues we said the soul, a girl, could travel
Anywhere, could read the hieroglyphs
Could dream the cornflowers out of nothingness
Could weather any temperature or fire
Bombing, could watch the death of any small
Thing we were metaphysical
When we were young like that.

Imagine this: that it is summer
In the Arctic Regions now. That all the ice
Has come down washing the earth clean
Of its hands. Even if I were alive
Then & loose in Dresden as a little girl

Even if I had lived through that winter
& come to the west to watch you
In white as you did your alchemies,
Even then I would want you as some
Thing I could write down, some palpable
Milori blue substance, a metal, a stone.

Kid Flash

Thanks for the comics.
I hate The Green Lantern.
I hate Kid Flash.
I put them all in the mess hall trash.
When I come home, I will need all new clothes.
These ones are all ripped up.
                    LOVE, HOWARD
                    JUNE 29, 1964

Born in the dark, you come back up,
it's a red thing, nightclubbing.
Once, in the Cat's Paw
I fell in love with each man at the bar,
their deeply flanneled arms, their slow bond
with other boys, their back roads,
the women they would never share.

I hate the day coming back
like the horn with its mute inside.
I hate the sheets suspect of tousling
by some other two,
the clothes that seem dampened
by some bygone decade
when you smooth them back on.

from A HUNGER

Into jazz which makes no children,
into the high wind of the boardwalk,
the aristocracy of a girl's free afternoons,
into the south of boys traveling,
the stucco motel with two-hour coupling shifts,
into the north of men drinking clear
water, to the cafe in New York
where the horn player is always hungry
sweaty, lit in red & you
backing him up, me
in the diamondback dawn, needing
all new clothes, born
in the early morning heat, back up
from camp, I think
I was lonely for everyone in the world.

Heartbeat

Let me be brief then
I will go on worshiping
the perfect mean lines, the light
on them visible only through the neon
signs of life, the parts which glow
all night when peaceful sorts are sleeping,
when the wanderers are still avenging
their insomnia in the dark
false hellebore red of poolhalls,
in the allnight pastel caves of laundromats,
in the wrong decade coffee shop in Ypsilanti
where even the manager can't lend the key
to the men's room,
                    I love
these things too, the self serve
filling station where a pale hand
sneaks out making silver
change, or the one dark palm
in the meat shop on Amsterdam & 110th
behind the curtain handing out
the little envelopes of *Heartbeat*,
                    I covet
these things too,
some third world after this one
& the one that goes hereafter,
in that world you will be important,
devoured by the fawns,
inscrutable Christmas rose, toxic
in your leather coat phase for a long time
worshiping the long blonde stains left
after light & after fire.

from A HUNGER

Danse Macabre

What the sailors thought on that last night
As they fell in little heaps on the deck

Asleep beneath the scythes
Of the Norwegian stars, adrift

Until six hundred years from now, their ship
Will sail back home, still with its cargo full
Of sheep's wool, accidents, the semi-precious
Spices of an Asian girl who ran away.

As if you wanted now to tell me after all
This time what Giovanni was about to say
At five o'clock on a Friday afternoon
As he wrote down his last Italian majuscule

In the rushlight of a sun gone
Rancid with indifference & fell

To a summer night when even the moon
Was a sickle of fire & a whole city kicked off
Its covers in the heat, on a night when bad dreams
Were invented & you gave in. Imagine this:

The last friar in the north of France, latching
The door to his room, leaving his shoes by the bed,
Writing it all down so you would know
Exactly what it is to trick oblivion.

What were you thinking as the ripe wheat stood
Uncut in fields, the peasants bundled in the streets,
The Pope preserved between two blazing fires,
When even the boldest wolves retreated to dark,

When night letters were sent
& never arrived, burning to speak?

What the Whales Sound Like in Manhattan

There had been some small confusion, some
commotion on the upper reaches of this island,
on the West Side where the sun was setting

like the reigns of emperors gone obsolete.
It was a sunset of a certain alchemy
of oranges with the blues of bruises healing.

It was where the river smell was slightly rancid,
slightly salted, slightly breathless & aroused.
There had been some wonderful confoundment

on the Avenue of the Americas, something
blocking buses & pedestrians. It was something
unemployed & elegant, it was a whale come home

for night. In Manhattan what the whales
sound like at night is blue & unpossessable.
This sound is something only they can do.

It is a sound that catches on the canopies
of pre-war highrise buildings designed to keep out
light & Latin music & the seeds of Chinese children

eating kiwis on these handsome summer nights.
It is a sound that tips the gryphons on the tops
of buildings, one that spreads the concrete wings

of gargoyles clutched to rooftops looking out
for seasons. In Manhattan it is not that common
to have whales. Bowing west, the Ming Men

take home their tangerines & porcelains.
Vehicles have learned to pass the thing
on Broadway, headlights bruise its hide.

from A HUNGER

The animal is spent & cares no longer
if the taxis honk or merchants or late travelers
take pokes at it. The stoplight changes red

to green resounding on the whale's great
shimmered rind. As an emperor folds
his napkin at the last meal of his dynasty,

luminous & moribund, inside the whale
the sound is one tympanic archaeology.
The bones are perfect as the gospel wind.

The Beginning of the Beginning

At dawn they are beginning
The small fires around my home.
I am afraid of what the world will do.
They huddle at the fires warming
Their hands, pawing the heat.
I long to come that close to flame.
As the sun spills out

This first extinct red light
I watch them from my window, watch
Them worship something warmer,
Much more powerful than I could ever be.
I am waiting for the season to give in.
I do not believe in punishment.
The world will rise by morning red

At the tips of its wings.
What the world will do it will keep
On doing. By day, I will be light again.
I will survive & outsurvive the hours.
I will have done wrong in my sleep.
I will have dreamed of fires warmer
Fires smaller, much more beautiful.
Far more hungry, worshiped, singed.

In a Landlocked Time

There is nothing like the mistral lull
of fishermen devoting days to the sea.
That is the kind of love which I require,
the forty years of worship for the weather,
the homage to the captured thing.

A year ago, I was preparing my body.
A scouring, the long oiled baths, the embalming
with fragrances & color, my long love of ritual.
When all else fails, you see me resorting to mythologies
& I become the Hyperborean that I am.

As of yesterday, it was irrevocably fall.
There was to be no turning back,
we were deep into it then. I am attendant
on this time the time between
the north wind & the present tense.

The landlord had tied down the trees, wrapping
their roots in canvas cloths. He put out
offerings, the bucketfuls of sand left
at the top & bottom of each set of stairs.
Even the salt air could not undo the ice.

He was preparing us for storm.
He was preparing for a time
when the lights would burn even by day.
In this small town, by winter
when only the warmblooded were left,

the fishermen could call out
of hypnosis the water-breathing
creatures which were slowing in the middle
of their tracks, their long descent
into a winter's night.

I am a creature of the real world, even
though you think I seldom choose to live there
properly. I am an air-breathing sort:
always cold at the extremity, never content
with the heat that I have.

A year ago, I was waterproofing myself
in virgin wool for the cold ride out
to watch the whales as they waited
for winter & hesitated, not too far
from land. In a landlocked time

I have never seen their great grey backs bending
the surface of the sea, never seen their cool reluctance
to stray too far from human warmth.

Lucie & Her Sisters

It's not enough to have my one dream in hand long after I am gone. I'll be a locust by then, learning in the next life how to fly transparently, how to deposit my old skins on the outside of the screened-in porch in some pastoral set in the last open space in America a hundred years from now. For now, I am transfixed by possessing the things of this world.

The littlest sister phones collect. She's run away from home, the first child in our family to be slapped in the face. She sleeps her first night in the Victoria House. She's too young to have a calling yet. Bells toll, the noon whistle passes over the town, over the phone like emergency, a slate cloud. Fishermen feel it on the bay. Lobsters stir in their crates. It is almost spring. She's seventeen. She says the town is like a stage set being torn down, a play that's had its run.

Sometimes I think the world's coming to end. Joel called this morning on his way to Halifax. His mother has a rare deterioration of the eye. She's losing the middle of everything. I imagine that she sees him as a mane of dark Polynesian hair, no features left. She lived her life in books, he says. Now she reads the white outside aisles of each page. She watches television through a round glass bauble, listens. They pick our softest parts to take away.

The oldest sister phones at the orchid hour of Southern California Time. By the time our father dies, we will learn to guard each other, vigilant. For one November day, we lived together in his glass home, built above our coal, at the crack of the highest hill of *Gan Aden*, a cove farm. An opulence in Ruff Creek, a miner's town, a bowl herd of Black Angus silhouettes, invisible by evening. Our mineral rights, curled in a humpbacked trunk in someone else's wooden attic, were never found. Someday, we will inherit each other. She will have her life in her hands.

A middle sister calls from Washington. She has a secret, governmental. It's too dark to speak of. The whole family could wind up back in Pittsburgh with an investigator parked in our driveway, surveying us, making his move to come in, to question us, to find out if any of us have ever lied. We have, all of us. It's too soon to tell.

I don't want to be around to watch them die. Tonight, one of us sleeps in the Victoria, old angels guard the wooden bed. The air in seatowns never has a chance to dry. Things moult. Everything is old. The mail is damp & old. I don't want to be around to watch a family dying off. I want to be the first.

Each plague species exists in two phases: solitary & gregarious. Bands of nymphs wander & adult swarms take flight spontaneously on warm days like these when the body temperature is high.

Two thousand square miles of green-veined wings, we cross the Atlantic & some get lost along the way as the cool air of nights at sea catches in our own wind, the wind we make when we possess everything in our paths in order to survive & feed. In a new century, I will be in solitary phase, dislocated from the swarm on a flight from the desert in West Africa to the New World.

There on the outside of the screened-in porch, I will cling, feeling smug but slightly maudlin regarding the publication of my collected work. It is nearly night. The dark beasts are grazing, digesting constantly, switching their tails back & forth in the faint wheeze of the warm air. A northern wind rustles in the meadow grass. Dogs bark because they always do in pastorals, answering each other like the wolves they once were in another life.

Sometimes, my heart beats too fast for its own folds. I am this, genetically. Ann sleeps the deep sleep of the near-redeemed; she has no veil to speak of. Julie sleeps easily with secrets; she wishes on anything, anything. Melissa sleeps near the sea because she thinks that, once, I was saved there, born into the damp air of an old desire to stay alive for anything, at all costs. I hear the weather coming on. I wake all night & listen to my neighbor's yard fill up with the metallic sound of snow in early spring. A globe of light comes on in their attic & some nights, you could swear that it's the moon. It's dark there, that dark. You can be easily deceived.

Elective Mutes

Nobody suffers the way I do. Not with a sister...
But this sister of mine, a dark shadow robbing me
of sunlight, is my one and only torment.
                                    JUNE GIBBONS

Tuesday afternoon, Broadmoor

I

In summertime, when we were little, I remember we
walking with synchronized steps, a four-armed girl,
we've got everything
the same. We were eleven, a shadow & a shadow
of her shadow. I am born
first & I teach my sister to be quiet.
Here's the secret:
One day we will burn buildings together.
One day we will set fire to great things.
It sends shudders down my spine.
In the heat of swing park, we will take boys
down & mingle with them in the brushes.
In a basket, we will float down rivers, Venus
rising infrared, you've no idea
what it's like to have this other
half. We floating like hot house
fuchsia, two Chinese lanterns
through the water edge, a bulrush, shooting
stars. I will teach you to be perfect, more
quiet. I will teach you to be hard high self
mutilating. We will talk patois, speeded
up 78 on the record player, so no one else
can understand. We do, we know
the languages of hemlock, jimson weed.
Sometimes, my hands smell like sex.
That summer if anyone looked at one of us
we froze, like girls made of bloodstone,
crackleware. We kiln things.

from A HUNGER

We love each other like we grew
from the same set of pelvic bone,
as if we were attached like clethra
flowers to their stems.
We're budding now.

II

We were sixteen & took to our room.
J & I are two coloured girls of history.
We do dolls, most are twinnies like we are.
I am the vicar here, the dolls marry
on the floor, kneeling on a red patch
of my mother's velvet dress.
We sing hymns we stain the hymnsheets
in the colours of medieval luminations
the colour of Mars, some nights bloodred,
the blue of Mercury, azury
like the sky lit up all over America,
a clear suburban summer
night & the lawnmower's stopped
& the swimming pools are filled up
with the bice of night
water, a town in mid-America gone
mad, deserted. Someday we'll live there
when everyone's gone to the drive-in
& blonde twins are on the roofs of cars
or lounging on their sunchairs in the dark, soaking
up their moon, all the convertible tops
are down & the speakerbox hangs
on the rear view mirror like a locust,
slow & distorted like that
& you climb in back to have a boy
inside you, that's what I want, on the back seat
sprawling in the noises like an animal
he makes, but you're shy, you're bourgeois, you talk
American which I sort of like but it's kind of sleazy, you know?
But me & Jennifer are up here in our room, broadcasting

Radio Gibbons in the gloom of an English outpost of the RAF.
These are my children now.

FROM THE REGISTER OF DEATHS OF DOLLS:
   June Gibbons. Aged 9. Died of leg injury.
   George Gibbons. Aged 4. Died of eczema.
   Bluey Gibbons. Aged two and a half. Died of appendix
   Peter Gibbons. Aged 5. Adopted. Presumed dead.
   Polly Morgan-Gibbons. Age 4. Died of a slit face
   Susie Pope-Gibbons died the same time of a cracked skull.

We forecast the weather from our room.

III

Dear Lord, you have no idea
what it was like. *11 June, 1981.*
I want a baby of my own, caged wren, tiny
trapped inside me like a blow of laurel
growing in a field, high & taking
from my own blood like an other only smaller,
someone I can call my own.
We to Welsh Hook & down into the barn
J's lover, Carl, is there he *broke*
my virginity tonight. She
watched us, there was we
& blackeyed broken glass fallen
from the windows & a wild bird caught up
in the rafters, couldn't find his way back out.
Shrike: hangs its prey on wire fences, thorns.
This is what it felt like: for the first time
now I am alive. We did it
to the Stylistics, J watching
then we lay down heavy in the hay, heat
sticking stalks up under my blouse,
strawflowers, a resurrection weed inside of me.
Smoke: indicates confusion.
Fire: desire for escape.

from A HUNGER

Shoes off, summer night, whole world
smells of fennel, all romance
from the Book of Red Dreams:
Arson: indicates a twining.
Bitch: flammable, a lover.
Nakedness: perfection, fire inside thing consumed.
Sometimes we even dream the same, get that.

I burned it down today.

IV

Without my shadow, would I die?
At school once, in a tuberculosis scare
when we uncurled our limbs for vaccination
ours were the only coloured arms.
Pink pink pink pink black. I love
flowers. When we grow wild we are.
No one can hear us talk, we mute we shy.
The other girls are none of we.

From *The Little Books for Little Angels:*

> It is Christmas Day. The TV's on all afternoon. Lassie, Bonanza, imports from America. It is ten years ago, I have this dream. There are five children, blue-eyed little angels. There's a bird on top our tree. The TV's gone blue, all the stars of the show are Twinnies. My father in his big old resting chair. Everyone's dressed in Victorian clothes, as if there's been a wedding. White gloves & something catches fire. J is on her knees. We've come home from putting flowers on our mother's grave. She isn't really dead yet, she feeds us blood-pudding for supper. Everyone talking with no vowels. It's snowing hard & our house is getting more & more muffled. I've blue eyes, covered with lace. J & I are brides. We both have this disease of the lung. We are inseparable.

We'll die early & be stars.

V

By the next summer, we'd bandaged our breasts
down so hard we could barely breathe.
High on vodka & glue, we both fuck the same
boy. Lupine, hawthorn, love-lies-bleeding,
small violence of scent.
Something like magic is happening.
You've no idea how much I am
she. I am she. *Dear Lord,*
I am scared of her. She is not normal.
Someone is driving her insane. It is me.
Tonight she wound a cord around my neck
to strangle me, *6 November, Furzy Park.*
She broke our ritual, she goes too far.
We take brandy from beneath our bed,
go to Gipsy Lane to walk.
Wolfbane, daphne, trillium.
Really it's more of debris
there than anything else, the river's drying up.
But tonight, everything is full.
It has been raining for days.
Everything is dripping
like pen & ink drawings, long & lean
as the blackened Modigliani faces of my sister's art.
We entice each other constantly
in these beautiful nights
after neverending rain—
 First of all, I wept to God
—when world is wet & shy, under the bridge, I hold her
head down under
water & I feel her thrash
against me, just this once, I murder her,
it's a once in a lifetime thing you know?
You have no idea
how much I love her, I am she.
Sweet alyssum, larkspur, yew.
We kiss. Monkshood, nasturtium,
forget me not.

from A HUNGER

I Wish You Love

Like Josef's skull ascending from Brazilian soil
On a twine, she rises from her famous white bed,
Exhumed by morning. I am hunted into daylight
When I wake like that, god-hungry, startled.
Now that my father is gone, he has gone
Luminous. *I wish him love.*

The late sun comes to my own midwestern heart
At evening. Nights now, the anorexic soul
In spandex tights slips out of bed with me,
Spreads her black acrylic legs, tendons
The color of an unreasonably aroused male animal,
Starving, always wide & wide awake.

I want movie kinds of kisses. Now Dietrich's dead,
I'm ankle-deep in melancholia again.
A man & his little girl on a stamen red sleigh, first
Snowfall of the year, both oddly blonde in the bare
Afternoon, downhill. In the matter of the breaking
Of the heart, we are easily fractured. *I wish you shelter*

From the storm, A cozy fire to keep you warm.
I knew it would feel this way. I never knew
It would feel like this. A man in an English stadium
Caught in a wintry patch of flame, rolls down the green
Of Yorkshire, begging for water, longing to be put out
Like a pinched wick, snuffed, an old horse gone lame.

This morning, half of the Rhine was declared biologically dead.
By nightfall, the eels will be floating face up toward Germany,
Lighthearted & unlovely. I will wait for you in Schaffhausen.
There's a puncture in the southern reaches
Of the earth's protective atmosphere. I'm trying
To be moved by this, but I'm more piqued by Rapture now.

No one will ever love you like you wanted to be loved.
Your new woman is Easy on the Eye, you say. Since this recent
Nomenclature for the Wind Chill, the world's a colder place
I think. Less than zero Tuesday night.
I'm the kind of girl who calls from baths in old extravagant hotels.
I think of ruined thighs. *I wish you bluebirds in the spring.*

I was drinking moonshine out of a clear cup. You Montana
Boys will marry one day after all, in small vehicular domiciles.
Nothing changes much. The stupor of these cold November nights,
A wife stewing gumbos in a crockpot. I will travel east to New Jersey,
Land of the Most Lovely. Even the dead want to go home.
Someone made them promises they couldn't keep. *My loving heart*

& I agree, Now is the time to set you free. When I got off
The tracks of a long afternoon into this turnip-colored earth,
You were drunk & down somewhere in America, your father in
                                                                       the deep
South, courting a girl still in a cotton frock this late in the year.
When my own father died, we buried him with a trout fisher's book
& we all thought we couldn't go on anymore. I can't take my eyes

Off the news. Planes pass constantly over the snow belt,
Even in peacetime & the roads here go on & on, unreasonably flat.
No one is baptized. After a death in the family
Gadgets go wrong for a while; it's nothing
You shouldn't expect, the near-collapse of anything electrical
Or bound by heat or light. This is the gospel truth.

In the evangelic dusk
Way past the Bible belt, they're killing off
Large common beasts, shackle & hoist method.
Don't you think they know what's going on?
All of those old prophets were the same: doom, doom.
But most of all, When snowflakes fall

I wish you love. Monday, after a long weekend, your sister woke
Tattooed. Small, softtalking at the hip, coming for to carry her home.
These things aren't revocable, you know; it's a graceful, toxic kind
Of thing, tattoos. *I wish her love.* I miss my man again,
Curious & passionate like Josef's bones arising after all these years
Alone & unidentified in South America. I bid this slim farewell.

Now Dietrich's dead; we turn left here.

Ten Years Apprenticeship in Fantasy

My Darling C,

There is something to be said for Nature after all, dusk pending, variable stars. I have had a change in luminosity.

All winter long, I've tried not to write to you. There is something too final to it I should think. First, news of America: the farmers are being winnowed out again. Now that I have cable television, I am in touch with the world. In the rain last night, rice went for twenty-five cents a pound in the midwest. Blacks lined the barnlike edges of their city, umbrellaed by eaves & politics & the fair price of near-proteins. I, myself, as you know, have been starving alternately for a decade. Everyone wants to know why & I tell them it's my way of holding the world back.

Also, on the evening news, I saw a six-legged steer. The father (his master) reports that Beauty is in the Eye of the Beholder. He loves that thing. Everyone wants to know how many hearts it has. Only one.

In the more immediate vicinity of my house where—you should know, it is just on the verge of twilight—I have courted this darkness lying face down into my hands all afternoon, absolutely loathing the light, doing Gestalt fantasies (you're allowed, I hear, to feel healthy in erotic dreams of submission), waiting for an orange moon to bloom into the nightsky, waiting for absolute quiet, waiting to get vulnerable again.

Where I used to live, the fog slid off the great bourbon-colored mountain to roost around my house at dawn. It was as thick as a religious cough. Here, cats come down the corridors of the city streets like the selected survived. No one is rich anymore. The extended family makes its comeback in the clapboard houses where all porch-sitting has been suspended until spring.

There's a big to-do about lymphocytes & immunities, what with all of us living so close together, the quick, violent, unapproachable deaths of so many of us here. The body's weather allows each germ to enter musically: ethereal, fullblown. Of lymphocytes, I imagine they are one-celled stars in the big liquid chambers of the body underwater: glowing & attentive, lighting the way as they linger in that great invertebrate chain of hankering.

I know you get depressed when I get all lofty like this. I've been reading the Romantics since two o'clock. Even the poets married. I find comfort in this fact, though it besieges me with awe. Those of us who are susceptible to weather might be marred by the great heaving effort of the winter as it turns.

As I approach evening I wait for the sound of stars crackling. I have never heard this noise, not yet. I imagine it is never cool there in the long, bright, monolithic hour of each star. It tickles me, actually, that this light received expired long before I ever spoke. Like this letter, which, if passed from hand to hand, will reach you long after I am gone. This moment will continue for as long as you imagine / *Me. Until the star goes blank & quivers / Until it becomes vividly cold / Possessed by an old / Gravity & falls.*

In closing, let me remind you of the Siamese twins separated not long ago in Canada. They let the little one, the concave half, be girl. Without her, he will skip quicker, eat more heartily, raise up his own kind & I think he should be given that one good chance. What better reason to go on living than to repeat yourself autobiographically? She didn't have that chance you understand.

from A HUNGER

I know the storm has reached past your knees by now & the electricity falters & the mail has become erratic & you're living on your thoughtful supply of canned goods. Don't let your teeth & hair get weak, as certain vitamins & minerals are missed sorely in a bland diet of single-minded sustenance. Pray only that the heat inside lasts until this thing has passed. Stay up all night if you have to, to avoid bad dreaming. It can hurt you & I need you. I am, as ever, yours.

And So Long, I've Had You Fame

How odd that she would die into an August
night, I would have thought
she would have gone out in a pale clear
night of autumn, covered to the shoulder
in an ivory sheet, hair
fanned out across the pillow perfectly.
Fame will go by, and, so long, I've had you, Fame.
From under the door, the lights leak
into the hall & Sinatra going
over & over in the bedroom on repeat.
I was six & you were dying out.
I was sitting in a sky blue metal chair
in our kitchen in the east
digesting the fact, still, of my mother's second
honeymoon & the man living all over
our house, that she loved him, had him hard.
The sun was on our kitchen table, lighting
the back of my hand & the headline
in the *Post Gazette* said you were done.
That you were dying
even in the hour when our neighborhood
went indigo last night, in the hour
when our palms were stained by Sno-Cones,
in the hour when Russell's father would take home

the bases from the baseball diamond,
then my sister & I would move like spiders
into the nests of our dotted swiss nightgowns,
in the hours of a windless August night
in Pittsburgh & somewhere
Sinatra redundant
no one lifts the needle up, he's singing
like an angel
all night long along the famous dusk
of the Pacific shoreline
as your breathing slowed into the sweetest
toxic nothingness, so long, I've had you, face
down,   *Cursum Perficio.*

After the Grand Perhaps

After vespers, after the first snow
has fallen to its squalls, after New Wave,
after the anorexics have curled
into their geometric forms,
after the man with the apparition
in his one bad eye has done red things
behind the curtain of the lid & sleeps,
after the fallout shelter in the elementary school
has been packed with tins & other tangibles,
after the barn boys have woken, startled
by foxes & fire, warm in their hay, every part
of them blithe & smooth & touchable,
after the little vandals have tilted
toward the impossible seduction
to smash glass in the dark, getting away
with the most lethal pieces, leaving
the shards which travel most easily
through flesh as message

from A HUNGER

on the bathroom floor, the parking lots,
the irresistible debris of the neighbor's yard
where he's been constructing all winter long.
 After the pain has become an old known
friend, repeating itself, you can hold on to it.
 The power of fright, I think, is as much
as magnetic heat or gravity.
 After what is boundless: wind chimes,
fertile patches of the land,
the ochre symmetry of fields in fall,
the end of breath, the beginning
of shadow, the shadow of heat as it moves
the way the night heads west,
I take this road to arrive at its end
where the toll taker passes the night, reading.
 I feel the cupped heat
of his left hand as he inherits
change; on the road that is not his road
anymore I belong to whatever it is
which will happen to me.
 When I left this city I gave back
the metallic waking in the night, the signals
of barges moving coal up a slow river north,
the movement of trains, each whistle
like a woodwind song of another age
passing, each ambulance would split a night
in two, lying in bed as a little girl,
a fear of being taken with the sirens
as they lit the neighborhood in neon, quick
as the fire as it takes fire
& our house goes up in night.
 After what is arbitrary: the hand grazing
something too sharp or fine, the word spoken
out of sleep, the buckling of the knees to cold,
the melting of the parts to want,
the design of the moon to cast
unfriendly light, the dazed shadow
of the self as it follows the self,
the toll taker's sorrow

that we couldn't have been more intimate.
    Which leads me back to the land,
the old wolves which used to roam on it,
the one light left on the small far hill
where someone must be living still.
    After life there must be life.

from
THE MASTER LETTERS
(1995)

*For my mother
Virginia Greenwald*

A Preamble *to* The Master Letters

I

Emily Dickinson left, along with her fascicles of poems, three documents known as the Master Letters. In the week following Dickinson's death in May of 1886, her sister Lavinia found these in a locked box containing hundreds of poems. Even though these missives were penned as elaborate drafts suitable for mailing (the final letter, for instance, was composed on laid paper, cream with a blue rule, & embossed with a queen's head above the letter L)—there is doubt whether fair copies were ever posted or even if they were ever designed to be posted. The identity of the intended recipient remains unknown.

Two of these letters begin with the vocative—*Dear Master*. The third is to a Recipient Unknown. The letters may have been written to Samuel Bowles, or to the Reverend Charles Wadsworth. Or they may have been to a lover, or to God.

These are gracious, sometimes nearly erotic, worshipful documents, full of Dickinson's dramas of entreaty & intimacy, her distances—the Queen Recluse, little girl, the mystic, the breathless renouncer. *The Wife— without the Sign! Betrothed—without the swoon.* Dickinson, a master fabricator herself, imagined or addressed her Master in earnest, & the letters, like many of her love poems, are unabashed & urgent "bulletins from Immortality."

Dickinson, in all her surviving correspondence, was not known to have invented *letters* as fictive documents. Yet these three missives maintain the lyric density, the celestial stir, her high-pitched cadences, her odd Unfathomable systems of capitalization, the peculiar swooning syntax, the fluid stutter of her verse.

II

The following fifty-two poems, a series of latter-day Master Letters, echo formal & rhetorical devices from Dickinson's work. The first three, originally conceived as prose, were intended as a specific & finite homage to Dickinson's triptych—her *brocade devastations*. But my original impulse—the epistle procession (that impure, irresistible form of prose which lies on top of poetry)—gave way to an Other, coupled, more sinewy form. The third form fashioned was sterner still, the Old World sonnet—but American & cracked, *the odd marriage between hysteria & haiku.*

III

On the fabrication of the Master: he began as a Fixed star. He was particular. Over a period of a year, then another, then more years, my idea of the Master began an uprush—he became a kind of vortex of tempests & temperaments, visages & voicelessness. He took on the fractured countenance of a composite portrait, police-artist sketch. Editor, mentor, my aloof proportion, the father, the critic, beloved, the wizard—he was beside himself.

On the Speaker: at first, she was a brood of voice—a flock of women with Dickinson as mistress of the skein, the spinning wheel, the Queen Domestic, composed and composing, as she did, from her looms & room & seclusion. Remoteness is the founder of sweetness. Raids on other work began—Sappho, Bradstreet, Brontë, Akhmatova, Plath. *When I state Myself, as representative of the Verse—it does not mean me—but* a *Supposed Person.* Then, a lustrum into the composition, I signed a poem—*I.*

On the fabrication of the poem (Ezra Pound on Robert Frost): *Definition of Prayer—Dear Lord, pay attention to—*me.

IV

In the early summer of 1883, Dickinson wrote—*Dear Friend—You are like God. We pray to Him, & He answers "No." Then we pray to Him to rescind the "No," & He don't answer at all…*

Carrowmore

All about Carrowmore the lambs
Were blotched blue, belonging.

They were waiting for carnage or
Snuff. This is why they are born

To begin with, to end.
Ruminants do not frighten

At anything—gorge in the soil, butcher
Noise, the mere graze of predators.

All about Carrowmore
The rain quells for three days.

I remember how cold I was, the botched
Job of travelling. And just so.

Wherever I went I came with me.
She buried her bone barrette

In the ground's woolly shaft.
A tear of her hair, an old gift

To the burnt other who went
First. My thick braid, my ornament—

My belonging I
Remember how cold I will be.

Also, None Among Us Has Seen God

My Most Courteous Lord—

The Teutons have their word for keeping Quiet which our blessing
Language does not have. To say nothing of—*Agone*, to say nothing

Of the monk who set himself ablaze, in autumn hair & all, the ravish
& the wool of him, the mourning & the sweetest smell of him
                                                          —Alive—

How did you teach the learning of this Holding & the holding
Back—To say nothing of—*Ago*, obedience, the hiding in

The feral peace of speaking Not, the root & oath of it—
Old as a prehistoric furrow horse abed in awe & sediment,

Curled on his runic side, in the shape of an O, broken. Wake
Is agape, an outskirt of agony, blouse-white & bad—To say

Nothing of the nook of sleep—which is a ravage in the chamois night-
Sweat of your raff & shames, the fevers of a minor fire, the rage

Or punishment, the *Agapé*, the kerosene & bone-red rag.
That was the best moment of his life. The burning down.

Rome Beauty

My mother says in the beautiful
Rome Beauty of my wild head—

She wishes to decore the one bad
Spot, the mottled mishap in the road,

Fawn accident, the one dun
Bruise & just that one

& I'll be beauty, whole—where all the demons
Dine collectively on game, the momentous dumb

Switching of the great silvery utensils carrying on
In the gentry's red lit looming dining halls

Like cervine tails twitching in bad weather—*Heaven
Paints its wild irregularity*—When hunger dulls

The peasants harvesting the lesion's fall, I will
Be beautiful, gazelle.

Unholy

late September

Dear Master—

Last night I slept in Mutiny, woke surrounded by the scent of citrus, just as day dilated like an eye peering telescopically over a rough sea of Sentimentia, spying an island after weeks on weeks of nothing but navy, an occasional predatory sea-bird, a gratuitous cloud, no noise except water & then after that more water—& spied land. When I was young I sold slow French kisses as dry goods to sailors—as some girls made madmoney in more genteel ways, I had none of this.

It is unfortunate, especially in this hour of the millennium, to seek the Captain's calloused hand. He is more accustomed to handling rope, rough-whiskered sturdy twines, the perseverance of the sail as it ascends its mast & bursts like a god into the nautical knots of ruffian wind. He is so less used to handling the religious limbs of women, their finer slender arms, unbaptized clavicles, spleening, the Hopefull countenance.

As I explained, there is no Harm in Contrivances; there is little left to speak of save the long Unarcking Moment of post-coital estrangement, the untwined two blinking into the raw mottled air of a dim bedroom, uncoiling like that, windless, little left to say in a Terminal Voyaging. Let us say, for instance, there are but six things left to feel in the world, six things left to put your mouth on: *Bliss & Loss*—for two, *Trembling & Compulsion*—four, *Desire & Disease*—you see? Gerbil! Noodle! Little One.

Do not think me, Sir, distended with self-pity; far from my own lean truth. It's this devil of the ventriloquist bending my lackey's back again. My voice thrown, my Other littler self on my own knee, practicing a sleight of hand, the tongue of the Inventor wagging the tongue of the Invented. It is true that each self keeps a secret self which cannot speak when spoken to.

Parts of the mouth are not clean, unholy by growing old I am afraid.
In the funneled obsequious rooms of each house, the sails go slack—
to nowhere; it is spring & nothing hurts so much as—*this*.

When I was sixteen & played Miss Julie for a year, he said: *Take the
broom*. And I took the broom. And he said: *Sweep*. And I swept.

From the Scurvy City,
very earnestly—

Your Scholar

A Brief History of Asylum

My innocence diminishes in the thrall
Of a New World symmetry, a burial

Grounded in the anatomies of Virginia's earth—
The wetlands filling in & shifting common

Wealth with soil, sprung markers steep
Above the fallen alder leaves, askewed.

Did not the eyes of Lunatics look
Differently? Somehow asymmetrical—

The white girl's odd black iris
Narrow, pupils belladonnaed wide, high

As a bird of prey crossing
The sky's staired plain.

I am angel, addict, catherine wheel—a piece of work
On fire spinning sparks from Lourdes to Alexandria.

I press my face against the Aprilled rainy glass,
Rose at the throat, rose at the windless

Porthole, radiant mullion at the wheel window's wheel.
The hunters pursuing & the hounds pursuing—

& I a Jew in a hoot-owl's rood loft—
Innocence diminishing at the speed of

A baying foxhound wild for hunger or for love.
In the troop, savanna, clan of invalid or swamp,

A hood of souls gone maundering, moonstruck
& medieval in the tower's eternal Method of things.

*And the night cold & the night long & the river
To cross*—trepanning the fissure—*caves of the Wish.*

At a century's torsion, they began the trespass
Of the cranium—lobation, incision, wheelworks

Stilled & listening—House of Some Lords. From
The skull's bony porthole, rivers unbound & ran

Out—mandate of docile, mandate of Sweet, no roaring
Subaltern pain. The temples—yielding, lamblike, mild—

Invalid to sorrow—right half, left half, limbic & all
For memory or love—I am subject, subjugate, inthralled.

The Supernatural Is Only the Natural, Disclosed

At your feet, I am a shoemaker's apprentice,
Toxic in a long day of fumes. I'm listening

To the fluorescent light come on
In April, flinging a hot white scarf

Across a month mottled by the chemicals
Of eastern standard time, in the spokes of wheels

Of hormones turning in an unseasoned sky. In a gospel
According to Hunters, you name your bird

Without a gun. You sit & watch as one does in the woods,
Contemplating prey, awefully. You have a heart

As large as a silver cleat, small thing.
I should have liked to see you, before you became improbable.

In your woods, I would not name the flowers—
They bother me, spicy & devout as they are, perennial & full

Of the pretense of sweetness & decline.
You dazzle me.

In the wilderness, the blacksmiths & the cobblers leave
Their machinery on all night, greased

By the nasty oils of midnight
Till the custodian slips off the switch at dawn.

Should you, before this reaches you, experience Immortality,
Who will inform me of the exchange?

I entreat you—Sir—in your next white wove
Missive to call my name—correctly—just

from THE MASTER LETTERS

This once. The continual misspelling
Is a form of sorcery, it smacks

Of heresy. It would bereave—
Your Gnome

Obsession, Compulsion

The Breath is as much of Mob as I can master, love. Steamy
It comes on the winter's windowglass in the shapes of the faces

Of philosophers, there Aristotle's white crown & brow blown
Like the etching of a hunting dog covering tracks in the snow

With his paws. I felt a quiver like the quarry giving in. I'm a drop
In a thimble of boys to you Sir. I am glad to be born, ungroomed.

Did I displease you—But wont you tell me how?
The hounds, let loose from the iron gate, surrender their miles

Of packed marks in the snow travelling—away from home
They follow my life like a fence through the yards of rush

Grass where larger, muter animals than they stand—hooves
On the ground's hearth—& bear it, standing still. I stay indoors,

The heart's clean home; a thought is fire's phantom snuffed
Last night. Obsession helps me up the stairs at night, past

My Father's door—I watched his breath go clear & thin then flicker
Out, in Indian summer near noon one day. Thank you for your

Affections, even Veiled; I am compelled to travel to my bed
Each night alone in down, scoured as a holystone, the hounds
                                                                                       gathered

At the gate outside, staining the snow with their treasure,
Their kill. By morning I will comb & curry them.

I will remember you forgetting & bear this, lying—down—

> *Would you but guide,   your—*
> *Punitive Divine*

Carnivorous

I was lying loose from God. Strange is it not best
Beloved, in the New World, in this skinny life,

Intemperate with chance, my spirit quickens
For the fall's estate. In India, the half

Hour is the hour, we were like that then—
Jammed wrong & wrong in the diurnal

Mangy chambers of our carnall
Hearts, the rose robes rustling loose as velvet

Curtains at the stage prow, passing
Into the strange salt air of an Indian

Ocean, hoarding kindling, heading
West with hours, later than we might

Have known, counting tins of meats & oil left,
If they should lose or last the night.

from THE MASTER LETTERS

To a Strange Fashion of Forsaking

late winter

Master—

I hardly know to address you; you are—a man? Anon to dust. *Warum bin ich ich, und nicht du?*

Loved—I think I may never have touched your linen, nor your skin. It is winter again. What with crimped winds & a small Berlin of snow, I think it will be always this one way. Soon, I will be travelling by train—through it. I am seized with a small fever now; I cannot get small enough.

We were all vaccinated the other day. Some of the others dreamt of cows, or lambs at best. I write to you from an hour of broad linguistic flux— dialects of north & south mingling, the iodine of the east diminishing, leaving its rust stain to the voice. In the frozen ground, the earth apples lie like unborn calves; you are older than you used to be.

I want to know two things by the next person who writes:
Tell me—*When,* & then—*How will it happen?*

I renounce Nothing. I am imprinted erotically with—One. I will need the scarf about my mouth to quiet me. I am overheated by hard riding. Dartmoor prison is a beautiful place to be punished in. So thick the deciduous rash of the woods—contagious as a small pox in a small city quartered—the language abandons rapidly to form new strains, resistant, unbridled like that, & not surrendering.

Forsaking all others—anon to dust, I will not marry. *Though I myself be bridled of my mind.* Horizontal, without sentiment, in a bed of clematis & not say nay. Storm excites me, *Schadenfreude.* Even anonymity. I have no daughter—now. My father died two times. I am an extraordinary I & not you. Is this what you may call suffering?

That is my charge—

Did Not Come Back

In the roan hour between then & then again, the now, in the Babel
Of a sorrel ship gone horizontal to a prow of night, the breach of
                                                                                           owls

Abducted by broad light, but blind, in the crime, the titanesque of
                                                                                            rare
Assault—we who have come back—petitioning, from the chair

Electric with bad news, from the stunning, from the narrows
Of an evening gall, from the mooring of an hour slanted on the
                                                                                         follow

Bow, she rose from a bed of Ireland like a flyted trout, a shiny
Marvel on the sailor's deck, an apologia—divining—

As once, as at a salted empire port, he washed
Her fleeted body & they lied, the best of them, the cream & crush

Of this, the madrigal & sacrifice of that, the best of them,
The slowest velvet suffocation of their kind, did not come

Whittled back by autumn, at an hour between thorn & chaff,
Not come riddled with oblivion, the crossing & a shepherd's staff,

The moment between Have & Shall Not Want, we who have salt
Always know, that we who have—the best of us—did not come back.

from THE MASTER LETTERS

And You Know That I Know Milord That You Know

That I had no idea I had been travelling
In the scrying light, crutched friar roaming

Snow-apple orchards every autumn,
Clutching the fireless stricken lantern

Of your feudal dark. It was not known
To me to stop there in the scarce

Field of the cold country, constant, Prussian,
Quickened & set the shunt lamp down:

The exquisite extinguishing,
The adumbrated thing.

In the monarchy of me, my ritual
& tinctured mouth, I had no idea that I

Had wandered like a torch-monk cowled
In the dulcet life—Deceive & now

Be done with it. Each night, you loose
Your face in the dauntless, dusted temple

Of my hair. Each fall, relentless, willingly—
You were numberless & kill the light.

The October Horse

I

Shepherd—Fasten him to the hearth
Of the house, the righthand horse.

Old Autumn, same rude ritual—hung on
The fir-tree on the last October night.

Old Autumn, rough horse muscle—Done
By us. *I had a yearning I could tell to none.*

I have been trying, since the autumn's
Wield, to practice a simplicity.

Coppers, brasses, rite encumbers me.
I am surrounded by the metals

Of the implements—steam
Of engines—long esophagi

Of trains, the coach inconstant,
Rough, the landscape immaterial.

I have been artless, since September,
To habit a rusticity. All my oddments need

Be carriaged by a hired hand.
I possess too many things,

Cannot be quit—acquiring.
Beside the river, corn will ripen

In the new rude moon. Sickle on
The crown lands, travelling.

Gourds will plump & wither
On the vine if unattended to.

Needs must gather the Kinds
Of grain—then thrash & winnow it.

II

Here, in the north, the horse
Stands still. Machine keeps

Its swallow in the dark.
The plough ox carries on his work.

Shadows ripen at the clock
By line by line by line.

Dwarf star stands still, hindered
By the things of me, his brief

Arms full of me, of injury.
The train keeps cutting the corridor

In weather against it, or
Neither Here nor there.

I've not a sinew of nonchalance in me.
I miss the weight of him above me,

Me on him, hands empty for an hour
Clenched, the brood of ritual.

Old autumn, shepherd, right-
Hand horse—with host

Or yet alone, in heaven or at hearth—
Some how or no how, I propose, Sir, to see you.

Gratitude

I am alive, this morning—
& am alive—numbed

By field gray halcion, dulled by the gift
Of boiling water, the freedom to descend

My own glassed stairs, to wind
The century clock, to know

I am old enough to know—a long time Ago.
I remember Everything, remember everything.

From me—Sir—you have memorized my gift
For blister & audacity. From you—a gift

Only of a mute, the null of the janitor
Sweeping alone at night with his orange

Push broom in the fallout shelter.
It is—*Only*—*Motion, & am dumb.*

Dull Weather

Rises, sets, by my own hand, dog days end.
Even my self reminds me of you.

I cannot refrain from Ruin.
You coach your boys to violence, even in peculiar

Heat. They are hairless, clean as copper
Coins made new in a New England mint, doomed

To be spent. Your form is
Neanderthal in its simplicity—simplicity is

Bliss. *This is the world that opens,*
Shuts, flutters like the lashed Eye

Of a porcelain doll set down in its humpbacked
Trunk—by September you were only Sleeping,

Only—Cooler, frost, in dull
Weather plough, do not fail me now.

From the Proscenium

early January

My Dear Sir—

The year thus far has gone Blank. True, it is a new one, but it is too cold thus far for any Weather to take hold. The high winds blow the pilots out at night & sometimes I have gone shimmering into ungentle sleep. I know you like to hear about my seasons here; it is one thing we can speak of equally.

Regarding my Tudor Disregard for the words which bleed out on me in ink—exhale & listen closely to me now or cut me loose. All gods secretly wish to be women—baroque, fecund, vulgar, sweet. It's an old script I read aloud & the theatre is empty tonight.

I play for the Balconies, all velvet-backed maroon chairs, slightly hyperbolic like a coast guard sailor calling out to fog through a primitive megaphone, looking out for One left by the wreck, still clinging to a cleaving rock. Rouged in the face so the facial features can be seen in storm.

How can something this Small take up such space? A Soul enters & a room fills with an odd light as if a lung took in the first Homely glint coming from the wreck of an Elizabethan cargo ship—till my heart is so Full as pure sail, I cannot breathe.

In the Heights this evening, the Grief Group collects in the basement of a bad girls' School. Charity, Hope. Not penitentiary, but more of a blind girls' home, basement of brooms & broom-makers where no one ever gets out with Sight.

Infinity is true. And that which cannot be Taken back goes on like a Sixth Act, washing over & over a tutored undercurrent off the coast, which circles, which gives in, repeating itself iambically like the pulse of every thing which goes on beating—

from THE MASTER LETTERS

Into the loams of night, like meat veins in a white urn, fashioned after the Greek, in the old style of the Old World.

In the rash of scarlet fever, in your scarlet dreams, all the stakes were high & the theatre filled with donors urgent to contribute to your cause. You kicked the covers off, febrile, aching in the thighs, uncovered your covers for many nights in the proscenium of your bed, until the fever broke & the chase stopped & the Weather entered the room to cool you, to come back to me.

A chorus on stilts, all of us long-legged girls chanting that way we do, all syncopation, all Grief. This scarlatina line. Would you remember me after a scant season of forgetting, the noise of amnesia when memory is an orchestra in its pit, lost on the page? The woodwinds gone wrong. The second violinist gone mad. The harp player Fallen, forefingers poised on the sheepgut strings, all bewildered, the pages disordered—into the dissonant Faith of a song transcribed in the wrong incantation?

Faith to you Sir; the bad girls weave by rote—even if they cannot see. Grace to you Sir. Hand for the Wife.

>Blue hat to the Sailors, who never give in.
>I am—
>
>*Your,*
>*Faithfull Friend*

Radiating Naïveté

I am a false philosopher of this
World, a steady congregation

Of one, nobody's panther, nobody's
Tinny cigarbox, nobody's violin, no

Midsummer naïf in Havana rain.
I am glad to see the summer dying

Off, the umbrage of the cornfields, breast-
High stalks gone brittle in the drought.

The headlights early coming on, dusk
Is an old adjective, color of the blind

Reading their prayer in pocks.
You should have been

A contender, a Canadian dime mixed
Up in our own, worthless & shiny, jamming

Up vending machines & roadside phones,
Old Indian. The harvest will

Be small this year & dear—
I'm nobody's truck farmer, nobody's juke,

Nobody's cold sweat on the wooden front porch,
Nobody's southern heartbreak hill.

I'm wide-eyed as Louis Armstrong when he woke
Moonlit in his darkened motel room: all

My white soprano injuries.
I am acquisitive, I pray

from THE MASTER LETTERS

Alone. In the ashes, nobody's isotope,
No glass of milk. Nobody's stained-

Glass messages, not the radium
In its dish, wide-eyed

As Madame Curie, lit
By half-lives at her hand,

Nobody's sin, nobody's white-
Knuckled god, nobody's humming bird.

Fair Copy from a Fair World

October

Master, my tinsmith—

Then there is quiet. Light scars like the foxed pages of an old germanic text; you mottle at the touch. *The light goes out a first time.*

The century—an implement polished by the scythesmiths; seasons heaving; hours blinding in a heaven of perpetual laboring.

When I woke stitched in the cicatrix of our fair drab bed, I was mute. A voice bound by the long worn muslin of a mortal work. I would want to marry now, as Thomas said again, the Absences. *I didn't be— myself.*

In the economy of a tinker's cult, the goldsmiths structure all their tools alchemically. There, they fashion needles out of base & metalled cold. There, where they invoke the silver eye, transparent thread threads through, one fisheye wanders like the fox light on the hard floor of the Friar's room.

At five they loose the coppery churchbells on the parish here. Sky the color of a seam of swallows rushing on this old New World. Color of thrush, color of thrush. Then, there is quiet.

Everyone is asleep, light metals, mender wandering. Needle, thread—were precious there.

Two ravens, travelling at night most times, in flocks, collect in the blacksmith's oak by dusk, their feet fastened to the branch bowed by their tinny weight, perfectly, like a fair copy of a document Done. I was facile, as you know.

Your Aff—
Scholar

His Apprentice

You did not state your price. When you took
On the post of schoolmaster on the final day

Of Lent, you punished your own. In that age darkness
Came on early, over the fields of bunch

Grass, wire, English rye, the brass bells
Of the high church chiming every hour, hallowing

You home for supper; when the young boys turned
Clockwise in their straw beds & covered

Themselves with wools & wheat, you came home
Before a sallow harvest to recite your Latin

Prayers in bed at night. This is when I dreamed
You centuries ago, on my knees when I slid

Your high black boots off & laid
Them side by side at the foot

Of my bed, when you wanted me as much
As promises & fame, the necromances

With the long gone, those who rose
Out of their stopped steps to come

Blink at you in the fire's leathered
Eye, when you harrowed the lines of the backs

Of the bones of my hand, the gold
Bunch of my hair, the alchemy of my merely

Mortal form, unspoilt yet
By stars, physicians, aristocracy.

You Can't Always Get What You Want

eve of November

Sir,

Light of your loins—I have been to the ruins & come back with art. All season, the pigeons have found their way indoors somehow, trapped in the cellar, soiling the floors & the walls with their exterminating terrors, blind as babies upside down.

I know you have suffered, Sir. Since September I have seen a buck pinned against the chrome elaborate grating of a German Daimler as it moves across America in the middle of a century. Of violence, my love, two nights ago the city of Detroit went up in flames, women's faces on the news railroaded by weeping, bloody town, a devilish night of bonding, the sharing of blood Promises. *All boys should be nicer.*

All blazing autumnal melancholia converges with the end of daylight saving time. A rain storm all night long—all carnage, all wind, all hallows. Soon the tubercular dusk will enter my chamber like a bloodcolored candle snuffing out, this early in the afternoon. There are no sorcerers left, only mechanics to fix things as they break down.

You get what you need. I am invited, with religious frequency in parking lots, to be Saved, to convene, to partake in redemptive ritual, to come back to the small circle of prayers. I go on, alone, ever aware of the great algebraic equations which keep this world aloft. The stuff which sets the neons wild at night. The dolls are rocked in their woven baskets, the demimonde of the nursery.

No baby yet. Starlings cross the highways in shapes of colossal ruins crumbling down. How long is an hour in an afterlife. Tea on a silver service, the girlchild servant devoted, doting on—

> *the amenities of dusk, the aristocracy*
> *of servitude, how long she has been in*
> *the orchard watching the light transfusions*
> *as the night quicksilvers—intravenously—*
> *a blooding opened from its vein to Air.*

Pursuit of Happiness

August

Revd Sir—

I really am sorry that you are falln out with the Spiritual World, especially if I should have to answer for it.

There were so many nights I sat on the wooden stairs of my porch & listened to the biremes of the crickets' wings rowing & rowing deep into the darkness. Down the long coffin of the Mississippi.

A Wilderness Lord.

As if the moon would be Full as a brain not right this Dark—which is true—wherever you are, a hollow legend or blue willow plate. Or wherever you have been. *I pray you—*

Will to meet me in the orchard's shagged or shadowed southern light, the low rub of cicadas indexing their oil & eventide, then I would tell you—everything.

I send a message by a Mouth that cannot speak.

A Glooming Peace This Morning with It Brings

The sedative of frost composes
Its infinity of dormant melodramas

On the glass. It consoles one,
The solstice of the hour's no

Apparent motion, standing still.
It contents one, the solace of

Form & phantasm, of sieve
& specter, root & disposition.

The difference between desire & compulsion
Is that one is wanting, one is warding off.

Consort—submission is a form of brawling
Of the hearts, & one is Sped—a stroke or flaw

Inflicted northward, southward, pardoned still.
A plague on both our wills.

Housekeeping

After the Zhivago of it all, the terrible sleeve
Of ice, cataracted, relentless am I now to weave

You through a season of small thaw, am I to hire
The grappling hooks to fish the winter's

Missing implements from the river's whipstitched
Seams, my self a beckoned pharos as I light the switch

In your corridor of kitchen dark. You have been outside
My body now. And the sled cuts the snow one half

A world away, here—burden beasts are dead of it.
The hoary load, metalled spoons on leather strops, the cleft

Of blade—forgive me for how long it takes to mend
The tear in the body's tailored skin

Like the Siberian boy in autopsy
Stitched shut at last, & asymmetrically.

Haute Couture Vulgarity

16 July

To Recipient Unknown—

I am moved, Sir, by the plangency of the hand as it curls out from between the bars to unchain its palmer's chastity, a mummer's wave to Media, the angst of evening news in the blackened blue horizon of a vulgar suppertime, at the long Holy table of austere woolly feast. There will be ruin in unwelcome worldliness.

Imperial wizards roam the south of things, white Trash Arcana, cleaning this pale earth with their long rayon robes. There is much to be said for shrouding—spells cast in the old fraternal chants, the brotherhood—no one knows the Riff, the tune, but they—who understand the incensed, the insensible, the Song. I have been unwelcome in diurnal worlds. These people immolate themselves for cause, & I am mere effect, no Flame.

In the pageantries of mystics—in the hereafter & the heretofore, the Schutzstaffel pulses like an insect swarm in heat—everything which has power is Rhythmic & plagued. Hail then to the arms & legs which move in unison, to those who sleep or fly by night, the syncopated guard which guards this land from any but the bluest eye.

In Tornado Alley, the storms come like holy bowling balls down a long beige lane, striking the Most Mundane, the Plain, the God-Fearing Simple, the Moonfaced, the Righteous, the Just Married, the Unfashioned, the Accidentally Aryan Kin. This weather—an unwelcome shaman, punk funnel, white magic, black sheep, all through the oat belt, land of a sepia retrouvé charm. *Then why not buy a goddamn big Winnebago —& Drive.*

You should be glad, Sir, after all, not to live near me. I have too much of the martyr, would set myself ablaze—just for the bright light of the fire, a curiosity, for a cause if I had one, a Flame.

Could we see all we hope, or hear the whole we fear told tranquil, like another tale, there would be madness near.

The church steeple of exact midnight, erect in the unheard of mist of now, too warm to be Real, the cat's low yowling, hellering in fight or Heat, in the mist, my darling, each of us will be taken to a corridor somewhere, one by one & held down by the wrists—Be Good, this will hurt a little, hypodermically. Be pristine in excess Rhetoric, vary the baroque of the High Romantic Tongue, regard the Nun starving for idea. There will be ruin in a new world worldliness.

All are very naughty, & I am naughtiest of all,
Ever—

>His,
>Penitent Friend

Toxic Gumbo

Am I to be a patient
Saved by the grave experiment

Of serotonins muscling
Through the old bulbs of the brain, lit

For a brief reprieve of something like a filament
Of bliss for a long light

Hour, then fallen to the hinter
Hills in a squall

Of chemical, the indigenous white
Trash girl, living south of the narcissus

Of industry, where, in a toluene alley
Sugarcane tarnishes overnight, hindering

The bricky cracker soil where still
Some okra grows & other aboriginal things?

In the Attitude Desired for Exhibition

At Lissadell I am the red she
Fox in habitat; Occasion—mortifies.

All afternoon I have prepared my body
For the body of none.

A red fox will be modelled
In the attitude desired for exhibition,

A manikin of faith, a carrion
Of coveting, & vixenlimb.

It was I in the excelsior
A bed of slender curving

Woods & wind, used for curing,
Mounting, & the like—falconress

Motionless
In her gravid nest.

> *The thrushes sing at auburn dusk*
> *Like parlor ornaments wound up,*
>
> *The boy inserting two glass eyes in*
> *His crude nightingale, for torchsong,*
>
> *Armature, for the carry & the carrying on.*
> *You can no more. You can:*

See—how she is
Poised—the right

Front paw aloft, it
Hovers in mid-air,

No gravity
Will interrupt her stance.

Age will
Not treat her kindly.

Like Murder for Small Hay in the Underworld

Dear One—

Uncrippled in the kingdom of petition,
I am bent in the shape of the bow

Arcked out toward the particular wound
Of the animal felled. In the tribe,

One kills for game, one feeds the spirit
Of the hunted one, before it passes on.

Sing to her, sing to her.
I did not go to it. I did not bring to her.

I did not nurse the deer on its side.
No maize or small hay, offering.

I did not send her, spirit, on her way.
What was it as I lay aloft face-up,

Awake & let me offer me, to you,
Afloat, aroused, I am afraid

To die, the wildering.
Repetition was my angel then, hovering

At my side like a Beauty growing old.
How simply at the last the Fathom comes.

Not captive, prey, not kill.
Do you know how cold I am?

I was a jealous angel then.
I am a jealous angel, now.

I did not sing to her.

Everybody Has a Heart, Except Some People

You have fed me on Air too long—a daguerreotype
With its ghostly subtexts of marks & jars—

There—the line crossing the brow
Like Anne Boleyn's clean cotton cap

Soiled on the day of her death. There the odd singe
Of iodine crossing the left hand, wed to mercurial rings

Like spooks—a vapor from another time.
Then—if your pleasure would be so—pleased—

Would you travel toward—me—unpolished & naïve,
Hammocked in a sling of madness as unjarring

As your hand when you wake me carefully
To tell me of the news that I have steeled

Myself against for a thousand mornings
Before this one?

Moving On in the Dark Like Loaded Boats at Night, Though There Is No Course, There Is Boundlessness

Master, then This—I crossed my father's gate.
Once, I walked into the northern lake

Dazzled by the lubricious feel of old botched
Leaves. When he died, he went on like a loaded

Trout stream—toward a Body larger than this one
Is, wading hip-high in the loaded

Dark of boneless water, moving On.
After Pennsylvania, I couldn't breathe.

Why would what died once keep on dying off
Over & over like a seam in an old velvet coat?

Every night I am the same brilliant fluke
Rising from my bed like a cut-

Throat trout listening for Trick, not
Moving, bound—& if you die of air as Well

The stream will sew itself shut—my lodengreen gills
Will be rouged past Recognition in a vein of metal ore.

When the boat leaves the lake stacked with odd
Amphibians tinned in salt, the metalled lids

Will glint like zippers, marlin,
Stars. In this half-lured life all

Night long I will listen for you, loaded
Like an ark, Boundless, Void

Of course—moving On.
How long how on how oft how long.

from THE MASTER LETTERS

Your Cromwell, Your Thomas More

In ruthless October, the salt flats dry out.
Meats will go bad; there will be nothing to Preserve.

Take your Wolsey, your Thomas More, your boys wrapt
In velvet, foxfurs & lynx, cloths embroidered from Far east,

Take them home with you & listen to their taking Heed.
Go in fear of the Body's uncial script, its scheme, its ruthlessness,

Its low river of sleep & wrongful dirge.
Which of us will be Mistaken?

I am detached from the Thames of mine now—look
That I lie Alone in my chamber, Solicitor, profound asleep.

I am chastened, misshapen wings. Or womanly.
Take your Cromwell, your cardinal sins, your Earl,

Your lord & chancellor, your castles marred
By arch & dank distress, your England, your—

Oblivion of rain, the luminous text, your trespasses—
Your bluster, blackmail & your witnesses.

I will meet you in the district of small Rain,
The fog will be lusty over & over again—

The great passioned Wether,
Who—will lead your salty flock astray?

The Four Last Things:
Do not listen to the hangers or rosins or lubricants of rhetoric.

Do not mist your windows over for the sake of untrained birds.
Do not look on Milk Street for our pleasure gone *to heaven*

In our feather beds, like falcon nests or beardless boys.
As for the dread, I warn you the dread is dangerous—

A man will execute his
Peerage when he dies—

*By the Hand
Off Hym whyche I trust shortly shallbe yours—*

I Dont Know Who It Is, That Sings, nor Did I, Would I Tell

November

Master—

You say I have Misenveloped & sent you something Else. In the middle of it all, my mind went blank, all the red notes of terror, blinking. Please to tell me—have I unsettled you by this?

I told Ravi that a fear is not a temporal thing, the moment—now, is Now. It is the next which harms him so. *I wonder how long we shall wonder; how early we shall know.*

On the moors, all the russet weeds have grown there—always, they keep on going on. The rainstorm happens helplessly, like typhus, fills the mind's eye like the vacant oil lamps lighting like a lung with ochre liquid when the nighttime comes on, helplessly. Who is to leave here first, hooded in a yellow cape? *Where shall I hide my things?*

Suddenly, I am stammering in the face of Probability. I thought when the sparse trees began descent, that you would come to me. There is the thunder now; it gives the world a rampant tinge.

He has, after all, an ancient soul; he is unbent by Possibility as he walks sturdy in the rain, steady as a metronome's pendulum keeping—Time. No slicker, no hazard, no hood. If I lose him I will be insignificant. *What a privilege it is to be so insignificant.*

Bliss—is unnatural—
Your, L

Grimoire

In the tameless night season,
The griefless wind, it is nothing

That I want. A beautiful fever
Took me down. Once, when the ichors

Lit the vein, the world was soothe & good.
I was at homeward in the murmur

Of the twitching hearts,
The old gone gods;

The replicative beautiful
Was looming all night long.

How many druid doctors
I have known & long ago when druidry

Was my first dream, debriding.
And all of the lexicons here at my hand.

And all the spirit-papers taking flame.
An ethery agonal of sooth & rune

And knowing—this—that soon
My little hook of incantation

Will be done. It was a magical.
And it is nothing that I want.

Work

Lord, one day you'll find these in a locked box, unlocked
By your daughter, who will roam with you to the fire-

Place & kneel there at another's ashes, scoop
Them out into a sugar bowl to take home with you to spread

Them on your garden floor, fertile enough for pale
Infertile wintertime. Kneel now with me while I am still

Alive & vivid, blessed by a season of high fever, still
Whole at the larynx & can speak these things

Aloud to you. For one season I have swept
A city by a storm. For you, love, my hair is famous

Hair, my hands are clean, large & white enough
For harm. At the throat of November, when the streets

Are waxy as the underbellies of awed swans, besieged
By wet, cremated leaves, an ancient light lights

The season in its ancient repetitions, old song
About the father, the bedeviling, the histories.

Historically, I am insatiable & cannot be beloved hard
Enough. I'm intoxicated, a little whore, lie

Now with me while I am still holy like
This: *I hid me*—as the lice hid all through the spring

Of my hair, divine in their guise, invisible
Cocoons beating white & more or less white,

Their bedeviling, as they hid in their cases
While I slept face down in my hair, white in my bed,

Little lamb, an innocent. I will harm as hard
As I have sealed the ashes in their urn, bold

As a tendon arcked in the lover's hip as she spreads
Her wing—you are impotent, you are wed, I am

Thinking of the humpbacked trunk, full
Of my things, fifty years from now, the terrible

Crystal of what she will find, your precious
One, your lamb. This is my work.

The Last Passenger Pigeon in the Cincinnati Zoo

An annulment of a species is as keen
As a monocle held up to the sun catching a page

On fire. I would woo you if I could, bend
Back open like a mythic baring

Bird, backed up against a hawthorn
Bough. This is not to be held against me—

*This mere yearning & fondness I have
For the Beautiful*—even if my labors should be

Unscored by your yellow eye, even if obedience
Should be taken as an anesthesia before imagination

Run amok, or sophistry—Angel, biscuit, nice little piece
Of traffic. Even if my efforts should be misconstrued

I will go on forgiving your
Extinction, your offense, like nobody's

Business, like your cassia carnations blooming helplessly
In April's carrion, in an onion snow when every wild

Thing is extinguished by the dog days of a season
Run amok. Once, the midwestern sky was so thick

With migrations, we blocked the sun, gun
Metal grey, shot down & shipped

To the city in barrelfulls. Our odd
Marriage is the moment of the last night

Of the last day of the last passenger
Pigeon who died out in a dull spring of 1914—

from THE MASTER LETTERS

The unreeling last survivor in the Cincinnati Zoo
At the beginning of your century, when you

Were unfading, beautifully. On that anonymous
Awkward strutting night, wheeling out of a city's silver

Midst, the last bird died out, monogamous & willful,
No survivors—there will be no more

Carriers with their small white billed
Messages. I was willing to wait like that, in the spools

Of decades come undone like button thread unravelling,
An extinctive case of an unwinding

Species folding, classically.

Everything Husk to the Will

I

And twenty-four wild Novembers, two
Times as long as I ever knew

Him, living—my father unlucky
In the little aristocracy

Of Homestead, beside a century
Of other Jews with ruined

Hearts, unblest by happen-
Stance. What is, what happens, what

Will be. Weirds broke him.
November I am all

Cold light, hard in the pure
Refine of wish.

In Yorkshire wind
Is word, tonight is keeper

Of the hoard, all these Angle
Walls, the black stones wedged

Against each other—yeanling
Herd, huddled in their same

White nulled dominion. To a bad
End, all—by weather, bearing, husking,

Lay. Worthless by winter, I am
All husk to my will.

II

And the nights there, Saxon
In their crudity—mistral, guttural,

Ruined by the masterwind. Inclination
Is a little aristocracy. Genetic is

Heroic in conviction, is
The keeper of the wound, a free

Will offering, turned—down.
As for the lay, it is a form

Of expedition, piratical, a pack
Of chalk & squall

& pillagings. I will not be Teutonic
Keeper of that wold, but fast

In the grasp of the delible,
Borzoi lean, wolf

Hound to my will,
My father follow in

The same white broad dominion.
If it darken if a shadow if

Obeisance if it ruin
I would be of doubtful authorship.

The Interrupted Life

about April

My Apparition—Lord,

In a conflagration of cliff-swallows, there is no President. How is it they know where to go, in what mystery of shape, how to catch Fire, who is to fly First? An attar of wind ransacks the city. Even this far inland, the world is powdered by essential vagary & salt.

Letters arrive all day, bearing bad news & Godspeed. Foundering sweetnesses, loons, nymphs chatting, offerings & antidepressants in lightless brown bottles, poesy from all the World, news from Calais— that he is trembling—seasick of the passage from Dover, supplications, the Drawbridge up forever from Illinois, postmarks of Hospital, Nilotic deaths, pockmarks of England where even the Blessed one goes on his knees—being bashful, one looks at the river, one never looks back.

What funnel, what trembling, what absolute Monarchy how—do the swallows know what shape to take, what supposition—their only elegance?

They hurt me;
I grow older.

Everything in the world casts its shadow constantly, constantly, even in the dusk at Istanbul. An apple falls in the night like a sleigh stopped still in snow; a cradle quits rocking. An apple falls in night. The cliff-swallows bank, ascend.

How Can It Be I Am No Longer I

Winter was the ravaging in the scarified
Ghost garden, a freak of letters crossing down a rare

Path bleak with poplars. Only the yew were a crewel
Of kith at the fieldstone wall, annulled

As a dulcimer cinched in a green velvet sack.
To be damaged is to endanger—taut as the stark

Throats of castrati in their choir, lymphless & fawning
& pale. The miraculous conjoining

Where the beamless air harms our self & lung,
Our three-chambered heart & sternum,

Where two made a monstrous
Braid of other, ravishing.

To damage is an animal hunch
& urge, thou fallen—the marvellous much

Is the piece of Pleiades the underworld calls
The nightsky from their mud & rime. Perennials

Ghost the ground & underground the coffled
Veins, an aneurism of the ice & spectacle.

I would not speak again. How flinching
The world will seem—in the lynch

Of light as I sail home in a winter steeled
For the deaths of the few loved left living I will

Always love. I was a flint
To bliss & barbarous, a bristling

Of tracks like a starfish carved on his inner arm,
A tindering of tissue, a reliquary, twinned.

A singe of salt-hay shrouds the orchard-skin,
That I would be—lukewarm, mammalian, even then,

In winter when moss sheathes every thing alive
& everything not or once alive.

That I would be—dryadic, gothic, fanatic against
The vanishing; I will not speak to you again.

The Sleeping Hollow of His Face
Will Be the Straight Pass of Surrendering

One day he wakened from
His Winterstunde of dying,

To the most gold rustling
Of impending end, from

His own head & was,
He said, to be quit

Of reading books & ever
More. A death is portable

Like an abandon,
You can take it anywhere,

A provenance of haemoglobins
& some fate. And from that

Tourneying, that day,
There would be nothing

More to crave & nothing
More to set the heart on,

No cumulus of knowing,
No rubricant of pulse.

Even I know this—
The eventual caesura

Of the hoarding in the sweet
Conservatory of his head.

And then nothing
& then nothing more.

Am Moor

Am lean against.
Am the heavy hour

Hand at urge,
At the verge of one. Am the ice comb of the tonsured

Hair, am the second
Hand, halted, the velvet opera glove. Am slant. Am fen, the injure

Wind at withins,
Stranger where the storm forms a face if the body stands enough

In a weather this
Cripple & this rough. Am shunt. Was moon-shaped helmet left

In bog, was condition
Of a spirit shorn, childlike & herd. Was Andalusian, ambsace,

Bird. Am kept.
Was keeper of the badly marred, was furious done god, was

Patient, was bad
Luck, was nurse. Ninety badly wounded men lay baying

In the reddened reedy
Hay of Saxony, was surgeon to their flinch & hoop, was hospice

To their torso hall,
Was numinous creature to their dying

Off. Am numb.
Was shoulder & queer luck. Am among.

Was gaunt.
Was—why—for the mutton & moss. Was the rented room.

Was chamber & ambage
& tender & burn. Am esurient, was the hungry form.

Am anatomy.
Was the bleating thing.

from
TROUBLE IN MIND
(2004)

For Lucy Grealy
(1963–2002)

The Halo That Would Not Light

When, after many years, the raptor beak
Let loose of you,

                    He dropped your tiny body
In the scarab-colored hollow

                    Of a carriage, left you like a finch
Wrapped in its nest of linens wound

With linden leaves in a child's cardboard box.

Tonight the wind is hover-

Hunting as the leather seats of swings go back
And forth with no one in them

As certain and invisible as
                    Red scarves silking endlessly

From a magician's hollow hat
                    And the spectacular catastrophe

Of your endless childhood
                    Is done.

from TROUBLE IN MIND

After Raphael

Perhaps it isn't possible to say these things
Out loud without the noir

Of ardor and its plain-spoken elegance.

First, my father died. Then my mother
Did. My father died again.

After the strange storm they were ruined down
From the boughs.

                There were apples everywhere.

I am sick of not loving and not
Sleeping well, of wanting spleen.

All the Suffolk sheep stand still, eating
More, becoming fat and

                Legible. Inside, the ice assembles
Even on the crystal of the long-faced clock.

No one can read incisions sanserif; I can.
                The ghostpipes bloom at night

When no one can imagine them that way;
                I can. I am awake

Now, I can see them heathering the moors.
                The impossible post-

Raphaelite world in which I live—*is true:*
                I was little; I am middle. Will I not

                Grow old, not final
As the broken pleated falcon's wing, not

Opening, and folding in
                              The smaller rain?

Leaflet on Wooing

Wanting is reposed and plump
As the hands of a Romanov child

Folded in the doeskin sashes of her lap,
Paused before the little war begins.

        This one will be guttural, this war.
How is it possible to still be startled

As I am by the oblong silhouette of the coiling
Index finger of a pending death.

No longer will
            Wooing be the wondrous

Thing; instead, a homely domesticity, constant
As a field of early rye and yarrow-light.

What one is fit to stand is not what one is
Given, necessarily, and not this night.

Still Life with Aspirin

There she was, the mother of me, like a lit plinth,
Heavenly, though I was reared to find this kind

    Of visitation impractical; she was an unbearable detail
Of the supreme celestial map,

    Of which I had been taught that there was
No such thing. Stevens wrote that

    For a poem to be true, it must "come from an Ever."
If you don't fathom that, then you should not be reading this.

    I was there, at Ever, and it was mostly poignant and it was
                                                                               cruel.
It was a subjunctive place where touch was so particular it hurt

    Like a veterinarian's deep kiss, like a Jerusalem somewhere
Between fancy & imagination. I was the procuress

    And the gallowglass guarding the history and turf of
                                                                                everything
Intimate. What word would you use to describe me now.

    Imperishable? Imperishable. The stars
Appear every night in the sky. All is not well.

    All Deepens. V. told me that. All deepens, which is
To say—nothing—like a mild analgesic, which is to say everything

    Like Lear's three girls. Which is to say:
All of my objects have lost their correlative states

    And you want to know why. Because things are just
Things now, just as everyone said they would be.

When I was there, at Ever, by the way,
I was an ascetic and unfanciful. The land there

   Was all as peaceful as an aspirin, as the West Bank
Is an eternal circle of chalk and bruise and war.

   You did not dream I held political
Ideals, did you. You should not be reading this and are.

   Remember me in the blowsy humid corridors
Beneath the Wailing Wall, most sacred place of all.

   Remember me: wishing, specific, marooned, as
One who knew exactly what the Ever was & is, a velvet school

   Of courtesan, a gallows bird, all deep, all deepening.

Herculaneum

No one is bored, just barbaric
Anymore. Ash admixed with rain, which cooled

The air. How much longer will this beauty
                              Of yours last?

As if even the idea of the city
Has been lost for twenty centuries.

Don't quail like this; go
Gracefully instead.
                        Eros enters

The room like a lesser god stopped still
In the middle of a bath of oil & umbrage in

The exquisite hour.

                        No one is
Exquisite anymore. The river is so small now

It will be hard to drown
In it. And still this world's a pretty one.

                        What world.

The One Theme of Which Everything Else Is a Variation

    Innocence is a catarrh of the mind, distressed,
As finite as the grade school teacher in Sierra Leone

    Whose arms were axed off only at the hand, first left
And then the right, and then his mouth as he was making noise

    And should be shut. A man can learn to speak again,
But never pray.
            Wisdom is experience bundled, with prosthetic wrists.

    I cannot master anymore the surgical or magical,
I do not know how the specific punishments or amputations are so

    Meted out. When you delete a wing or limb
From a creature's form, it will inevitably cry out against this

    Taking, but in the end it will become grievously docile,
Shut; far gone old god, you have been plain.

    Let me list here the things I wish to bring with me,
For the life after this or that. I will not go back the way I came,

    Carrying my clay Picasso and my tin of ginger,
Flying toward home on my way away from home.

    If I am lucky in this life, here, I will go on
Being whole, and speak again old god, I will be plain.

Periodic Table of Ethereal Elements

I was not ready for your form to be cold
Ever. Even in life

You did not inhabit, necessarily, a form,
But a mind of

Rarer liquid element. It had not occurred to me
You would take

Leave and it will be winter from now on, not only
Here, in the ordinary,

But there too, in the extraordinary elegance
Of calcium and finery

And loss. Keep me

Tethered here, breathtakingly awkward and alive.

If you had a psyche it was not known to me.

If you had a figure it would be heavy ivory.

If you were a man, you would be

An autumn of black carriages filled red with leaves
From sycamore trees,

Not scattering. I was not ready for such
Earthward and unease.

Goodbye to the imperium, the rinsing wind. You, cold
As God and the great

Glassed castle in which I've lived, simply
Now a house.

A girl ago, a girlhood gone like a phial of ether
Thrown on fire—just

A little jump of flame, like grief, or,

Like a penicillin that has lost its skill at killing
Off, it then is gone.

Some Details of Hell

It is time now to turn off the devices in the wing
And listen to the rain. It is time, now, to sit still

And run your finger along the suprasternum of
The truth as it arches above the viscera, and finally.

It is a time when wires & catheters marked "single use"
Have most certainly been used before: cleansed

And sterilized, but having spent time in someone
Else's heart, they have been contaminant and

Ruined. I was strong and could lift half
Of everything. I was powerful and could be alive

And lithe as tiny scissors used
To cut out tissue in a human which had gone wrong.

Hell is a world of its own, with its own
Towns and country-side. There I stayed beside your nearly

    Warm-blooded form like a brook mink in the clutch
Of a slightly larger animal and sat still, having

    Spent a moment in someone else's marrow,
A diaphanoscope, catastrophic as the good love

    Of a tea-stained bride abroad in the rain
Of saxifrage and clove, tomorrowing.

Basic Poem in a Basic Tongue

Here is the maudlin petty bourgeoisie of ruin.

A sullen pity-craft before the fallows
                Of Allhallowmas.

The aristocracy in one green cortège
                At the registry of Vehicle and Animus.

A muster of pale stars stationed like gazelles just looking-up,
                Before the rustle of the coming kill.

At home, the hoi polloi keep tendering the books of Job's
                Despond, in braille.

The girl at open half-door in her early Netherlandish light
                Of melancholia.

So many brooding swans like floating inkstains on a lake
                Of slender wakefulness.

Death as a German Expert

                                  The North Star hanging
Like an umlaut over all of us, causes (even brittle) me to bend.

The weight of everything, bleak as babies in baskets
Rushing down the River Sauer toward their celestial misery.

I remember everything; my sister and I calling our mother person-
To-person in the afterlife. Always the dead will be lined as sad

And crookedly as fingerling potatoes in root-cellars dank enough
For overwintering. In Luckenwalde a young girl slides a needle

In the turnip-purple soft fold of her inner arm and this, too,
Transfigures to a kind of joy. Expertise is everything.

Angel, extinguish the tallows of the elder trees. (And he does.)
                                                             Death comes

Like another spotted foal born on the barn's cold floor,
Spindling to stand, and he does.

Gamine

Heart, be clean. Fists, be open, numb.
       Most lovely

Lovely, let me be wrong in almost every
Thing. That the page is waste, all that rag

Content. That even despairing relentlessly cannot

Spare you what you fear the most.
         Gamine, you are growing

Old now; it's your time. If you wait here
For the noises of this night,

They will sound out as the rustling of autumn,
        Spiky, dried of unctuous

Airs, blazing like a chestnut horse on fire in
The padlocked barn;
        It is time it will be time.

Morgue Near Heaven

If I imagine him healthy in his distressed
        Leather coat on someone's Sears plaid
Couch some years ago, then I will know
        All the nouns for shame he knows.

Perhaps I will write *green* as many times
        As he; he is affectionate about the spring;
I dread it as I dread the sulky pull of the season's
        Needle in its vein, drawing in.

I love him as I love all of the Dakotas,
        The two of them to which
I've never been, just as I've never really seen
        A death mask of his face,

Because, technically, he's never been
        That way, not yet.
If I keep his small triangle of a letter in his own
        Hand close to mine, then

Maybe I'll inherit all the Teutonic sentences
        He knows by heart, or all the same,
The grammar of the night, the factory
        Of slandering and fame.

The Insignificants

Tell me the story now in such
                      A way that I can hear it and still

Catch my breath. Rage is an aneurysm of the old animal
Brain, the reptilian gorge where nothing counts

But the body's urge & its boudoir
                      Of sulk and felt and shame.

Tell me I have heard tell there is a city
Where the graves float on the inconstant rain

Not fanciful, but accidental, actual—like milkstone
Spirits perched atop the smallest unbound human

Forms who died as insignificants.
                      For me, it is too late in the story

To die young, or guileless. I'd wanted once to love
Your mouth on mine, its ether

                      Gasping through a gauzy
Metal mask; I'd wanted to be breathed and taken

To an actual, like an addict floating on a desperate tiny river

Of open iridescent pigeons' wings and the floating poplin

                      Smocks of dusky, spoony girls.
As if I could breathe still.

A Lion in Winter

As long as the lions are rampant, I will stay
With him.
        As long as the clouded leopards

Surround the clouded bed with their gold & cirrus
Air, I will be there too. I was reading

When the winter shooed-
Away the fall and whitely lit the oil lamps of early

Dark. The night was turret-shaped in childhood,
        A bunch of mint and mane and swale.

What will I be when he is husk
To himself,
        Some flax or ghost of lynx in later winter light.

Boy at the Border of His Own Allegory

A boy phones from a Frankish-
Speaking manor in Flanders, in the rain,

      To tell me he has a shotgun
      Muzzle to the inside

Of his Romance-speaking
Mouth. I tell him, take it from that ragged

      North Sea lair and put it to
      The milk and honey coffer

Of your chest and hold it silo-
Still and reddening there.

      It isn't speaking that you wanted to be quit

      Of, but only just to stop the sadiron

      Heavy flooding of the figure

      Of your inconstant, northing heart.

Like a madrigal, a pastoral
In the pocket of my houndstooth vest,

You are the only beauty in this
Celestial torture I will call my own.

Still Life with Feral Horse

It is love and its relinquish
I am discussing here,
A sorrel horse loosed

On a salt marsh island
Pelted by high storms,
And furious. He will not

Be handled by human
Hands, not in this given life
Of gratitude and tallow lamps

And famous churlishness.
I have heard tell
That you know how
To kill a man.

Soul Keeping Company

The hours between washing and the well
Of burial are the soul's most troubled time.

I sat with her in keeping company
All through the affliction of the night, keeping

Soul constant, a second self. Earth is heavy
And I made no wish, save being

Merely magical. I am magical
No more. This, I well remember well.

In the sweet thereafter the impress
Of the senses will be tattooed to

The whole world ravelling in the clemency
Of an autumn of Octobers, all that bounty

Bountiful and the oaks specifically
Afire as everything dies off, inclining

To the merciful. I would have made of my body
A body to protect her, anything to keep

Her well & here—in the soul's suite
Before five tons of earth will bear

On her, stay here
Soul, in the good night of my company.

Self-Portrait with Her Hair on Fire

Now, it is as dark as the pathos of pushing a wheel-
Chair through the museum of a great metropolis.

I cannot tell you this, not now, not ever, even
In the letter I have written that is so epic

That if you were to open it, the pages would sail out
In the wind like confection moths being born

In the thousands out of their sacks, blowing
Away, page by page, in a wind the color of her hair

Across a medieval pillow endlessly scorched,
The singe of something living tinged with fire.

I will go on loving as I love the backs
                Of things and the invisible,

As I love the hideous or an attention
                      So attentive it is next to worshipping.

The Deerhunting

We were preparing to miss our President and his
                    Long resplendent, minky hands when

He is gone, when we will rue prosperity & youth blown
                    Off like a bard traipsing past

                    Dusk under a hunter's moon.
Regarding suffering: if it is all technique

                    And not a drop of substance,
Don't bother coming home. The last owl of

October was perched here, on the tiny antler
                    Of my dream, obsolete as a flintlock

Gun, and camouflaged by the wisdom
                    Of a jumpy age. In the chat room

Of your fluorescent orange imagination, you will
                    Find me lying in

                    The saddle between two saw-
Tooth mountains like a swamp deer

Out of bedding, in the rain. Regarding rain:
                  I hunt for it, its rut & arch, its tracks

That splash the slippery creek past weepy
                  Willows near the slough.

And by winter, our new President will be muzzle-
                  Loading the wrong dark men

                  In a long dark jerrybuild of robes.
Even the fawn bag limits have been reached,

                And the lung shots shot & the harvesting
Of fallow deer will be done by Tuesday night.

By November, the tines of my deepest thoughts will be "in
                Velvet." And I, the mother of nothing, mother

Of nothing at all, will spook, be
                Loving still, but just the same, the same.

Darwinism as Spite

The heart is a place made slippery
        As a minnow confused out

Of its school and caught on
A plaid pink dishtowel forty years ago

In Canada, startled as a hood-shy
            Falcon seized in

Flight, bewildered as a mine pony
            Sudden, taken up

From an underground of shale
Into the hinter of stark light,

Blinded by an eye accustomed only to
An underworld of bower, lake, or coal.

        Why was none of this written down?

from TROUBLE IN MIND

Lady with an Ermine

    In the snow, white noise, a gathering
Of foxes oddly standing still in the milk broth of oblivion.

    In the keep at Castlestrange, an ermine pelt in the shape
Of an ermine animal, but empty, slung over the carved

    Oak chair, carelessly & keeping no
One warm.

Fragment on Dissembling

    Curious in your dark
    Frock-coat, do everything
    That you have to,
        If it is time;
        Leave nothing
    Still unsaid.
    Once, to make of nothing
    Something, was divine.
        To have made
        Of something
    Nothing, was sublime.

The Halo That Lit Twice

Tell me where in what penultimate white
World do you imagine you can be quit

Of these
Blood-tied arteries which lead

Directly to the improbable thoracic
Cavity of me, what Department of Erotic

Wars, what Alexandria, what character-is-fate, what coven
Of intensive care, what raven-

Width, what upper GI bleed, what chamber
Of anatomy, what ice and vigory,

What breastplate, lymph, what coat
Of arms, what curious unspeakable, what one lamp left

On in the vaulted amber window of the Public Library
Where a cowled friar has been deep in study

Lucubrating like the patron saint of random births
And worthlessness,

An accidental light left all night
Long, pulsing slightly

Like the bundled one-ounce heart
Of an infant harvested, delivered here on ice,

Which began to flutter faintly
Like the halo that lit twice,

That lit and faltered, halted, lit
Once more, and then went out.

from TROUBLE IN MIND

Self-Portrait as Kaspar Hauser

What was it like then?
    In my prison I thought of nothing.

What did you think of?
    Not boot or trouser, not the bearable
    Light or trough, not rain,
    Not bread or wagon, water, rain.

What was it like?
    The heart had I known I had one had folded
    In. As if an ox lay down in rue & hay.
    I lay still.

What did you think then?
    I was a scar. A scoop of swale.
    An applecart left out in an orchard.
    It is December now. Nothing.

Could you speak then?
    The white of the paper blinded me.

Could you speak aloud?
    I was a wonderment.

Were you able to speak?

    Once, I felt a joy. This was as old as beasts
    Of burden working, in the grainy field.
    A plough of good white speech.

There was a toy in the shape of a small
White horse. It was to me a living form.
I was its equal, grief, the same grieved

Thing, wheeling & unworldly, wild as
Wheat. I will to be wandering in
The waving fields of eel-grass, as if

Underwater in the salt marsh of the moors.
A hatchet, flowering; a balky calf. As I touched
The flame I did not know how to flinch, but cried.

Self-Portrait with Self-Pity

        In the principalities
Of desire, retention of power

Is everything, even at the cost of treachery.
        I know this much as one

Familiar with the jack-keeping off
Of the barbarians outside the city's iron gate.

        I'm telling you, my bleak, all
        Winter long, it will be mercilessly

Iced here now, the frost is cold-cock
Cloven vixen prints on metal railroad tracks,

        The trains go on and on
With their whistling, with their tupelo cargo,

        Their serious & pitiless,
        Their limber want, their gloom.

from TROUBLE IN MIND

Girl at the Border of Her Own Allegory

A man takes off his armor past the Iron Age
And it stands without

      The man inside;
She folds in

The metal garments of his great blank
Wings of winter. In

Saint Petersburg, the night-
Engraving churchbells toll and in this

Constant cold I do not know
If tolling signifies

A death or marrying, hollowed
Out of frost, or rue, or injury.

      The dark is big, filling
      The city with silver

      And trouble. You are colder
Where you are,

Love, curious as the alchemist who keeps
His salamander living in a flask of fire, while

The will of me, a black reptilian
Doctor's bag, clicks shut.

                        My own fealty galls,
Bewilders me.

In Cocteau, to La Bête's white horse, the Beauty says:
Go where I am going. And he takes me there.

Of the Finished World

Open the final book: November spills
Its lamplit light, the clenched astronomer

Hunched at table, considering his vexed
Celestial map, illegible as the flinch

Of needles falling on the blanched
Rye fields in pentagrams.

The harvest is done with itself, its ransack
Done. The wild-coated horses bunch

In the clot of darkness that falls on the land.
In the twice-ploughed field, picked

Clean, what is left of the bottle-gourds
Will freeze by night, a throttled hour

From here. On the freighted road, laden with
Old hunger and apocrypha, a heaven sloughs

Its midden things, things left of the unfinished
World, its most hideous & permanent

Impermanence. I was not awake
For any war to speak of.

     In the finished world
I will be wind-awry, will be out

     Of mind, in asylum
Where even the astronomer will no longer

Attend to the world undone.
How have I lived here so long?

In Elsinore

There would be a boy

Insensible in fog
On an afternoon when lamps are hung

Even in mid-day

For the sake of those still travelling.
There would be a stray

Of music fashioned from a horsehair

Bow drawn across the torso
Of the cello's form.

In Elsinore where everything

Is probable, he would not die there
Like a child

But like a child he had wished to die.

The tide moves deeper
In and handsomely as Denmark sleeps

Collectively in wool.

For the sake of those still travelling
Who live so far & crookedly from

Here, I would not stay strangely

Like a child,
But like a child I have been astray.

Spain

The god-leash leaves
Its lashes on the broad bunched backs

Of sacrificial animals. The whippings stain

Even the muslin of the streets with bright red poppies

On this Sunday morning when the wedding

Would have been as full-blown as the cotton crop
In the hour

Before it's plucked from its scratchy little hulls.

I can say "little"

Now as many times as I goddamn
Want, here in the hour of my forty years & four,

Here beneath the hardback hour of my death or
Past as it will *really* happen here,

And then the saltwater's salt and its "heal" and sting,
This unholy lovely strapping

Thing, annulled. You will find me then,

A little damp, in

My small Madrid of shame.

from TROUBLE IN MIND

Portrait of Lucy with Fine Nile Jar

My torso is a cedar chest in the brief closet
Of the middle of a country, hollow

                Until three young sisters
Curl there like marsupials and shut

The bevelled door and die there,
                Not determined yet, into

The camphored pouch of an Otherworld.
Around this death there was a fine Nile jar

Of halo-light, where I am
                Thinking of you now,

                Everything; you're all
                Over;

Out of time like a nightjar
In the diorama of the great hall

Of prehistory, depicting the tiny cataclysmic
                Moment of some mythic, leggy

Accident that changed the world
One day, numinous as a Petrarchan

Sunflower in the night. A moment
                Perfect as a bee suspended

In the perfect weather of a honey jar.
Your heart was cinctured, full, surrounded

By a hinder of restharrow
                Roots, nestled in its little parasol

Of amber grief, willful as a wooden tiger standing
                In an empty yellow room.

While you were leaving, I was lying, eastward,
On my back, like a pharaoh counting

The layers of muslin wound
Around my cumbrous (nearly human)

Hand, counting the days until
                An evermore arrives.

from TROUBLE IN MIND

The Identity of the Bridegroom

One night you will walk into a flume
Of the great Mississippi River with your blue

Malthusian urge, in a gluey
                Great-coat of a great

Inertia, and go down into the runnelled
Underworld, standing still as a pale suitor

Handing blossoms to a girl with queen

Yellow jackets in her hair I swear
You will. I am tired

Of women who are sad. I am tired
                Of men who are tired.

You are unwholesome mantling
The river in this
                Ochre-wedded light.

Self-Portrait as a Herd of One

The reason why I love the orchard is my propensity for lavish
Order in certain seasons of the year, when a Glaswegian

Gloom ascends as snow apples fall long before the snow is
Come. When she died, it might as well have spooned the quince-

Shaped heart from me. Forgiveness, in this agnostic time, was
Not a possibility, the way each pome-fruit orchard was

A whole tin bucket of despairs, singly as benign as
Silvernerve, in accumulation something powerful and poisonous.

A hearse moves through the city like a herd of
One, bison-like and woolly in the summer sun, carnivorous.

Recall the kitchen and your half-learned love, the room you know
She will never be inside again, and someone telling you:

She is not here, she is not anywhere, you see, and you were there;
It was the last time you would be at home, in harm.

Physicism

In the valley of the Euphrates, each
Of the stars had certain shepherds

To the people there. Here, in this small valley
Showered with emboli, we each have none.

Before the Babylonians, the sun was called
Old Sheep, the planets Old Sheep Stars.

There are blood-sheep everywhere,
But no shepherds left.

                              Only blood sisters here,
All with the color taken from their sight.

We live in black & white, material
And motherless beneath the concavity of sky.

Phenomenal on the long aortic pulse
Of equinox, a Sumerian describes his stars

Collectively as *flock* and it is heavenly to him.
Here there is no heaven here.

Self-Portrait with Her Hair Cut Off

Like the Shropshire clock with its pocked off-white face
        Of Roman numerals as it wound down, the night will

Be as still as the garden of wildflowers and pinking
        Shears I wandered into once that many years before all

My hair was scissored off for punishment, a love so struck
        It might have slain you with its magnitude: the sack

Of dust called "Long Ago."
        In the pillow of swill I call "Now,"

The past happens over and over again like a kingfisher
        Veering off its destined course, and hovering.

                      Promise yourself just this
One thing: do not strive to be exceptional.

There will be hours for that in the hackneyed
        Looming after, and the afterwards.

from TROUBLE IN MIND

The One Thousand Days

There is the mourning dish of salt
Outside my door, a cup of quarantine, saucerless, a sign

    That one inside has been taken down
By grieving, ill tongue-tied will, or simple illness,

              Yet trouble came.
I have found electricity in mere ambition,

    If nothing else, yet to make myself sick on it,
A spectacle of marvelling & discontent.

    Let me tell you how it came to this.
I was turning over the tincture of things,

    I was trying to recollect the great maroon
Portière of everything that had ever happened,

    When the light first stopped its transport
And the weather ceased to be interesting,

    Then the dark drape closed over the altar
And a minor city's temple burnt to ground

    I was looking to become inscrutable.
I was longing to be seen through.

    It was at slaughtering, it was at the early
Stain of autumn when the dirt-tinted lambs

    Were brought down from the high
Unkempt fields of Sligo, bidden, unbidden, they

    Came down. It was then that I was
Quit of speech, a thousand northbound nights of it.

        Then was ambition come
Gleaming up like a fractured bone as it breaks

        Through the bodiced veil of skin.
I marry into it, a thistle on the palm, salt-pelt on

        The slaughtering, and trouble came.
That the name of bliss is only in the diminishing

        (As far as possible) of pain. That I had quit
The quiet velvet cult of it,
                        Yet trouble came.

from TROUBLE IN MIND

Dire Wolf

Sorrows, like a gathering of dire wolves, come in packs. To you,
I am not speaking anymore. Whom

Shall I address?

Now that you have gotten these things off
Your barrel chest, it is time for you to merge into the sobbing

Rain, like a one-room scene in Appalachia, smeared
By fog. I adored you as much as an aluminum

Bucket of storm after
A great unlovely silvered thirst. How

Nice for me. In the Pleistocene, the wild wolves roamed
In scattered sorrows over

Everywhere, prodigious in appetite, howling
At the hollow of

Everything empty like a throat coated
With the fabric of a bolt

Of red. There

Are things which can dismantle entirely
A spirit, such as the pathetic maledictive fear

Of loss. Of loss:
You get to speak of it, once

You are its intimate, and not before; it would be
"Appropriation." But in the great white rendezvous, where

I was brooding
Just a while, you get to speak of dire love.

Pamphlet on Ravening

You cannot will intoxication, vertigo, a ravening or wild
                Love. Of wisdom, I have plenty,

Like a keep of potted meats before the blizzard comes.
                    Of sweetness, I've a bowl of plenty too,

Though it's against the law to harbor wonder

In the prison of the Post-Hellenic world where
                I move easily
Miraculous and moving

                  On the slower barge
Up the River Hubris in the post-curiouser world.
                            Wondrous:

I was a hunger artist once, as well.
                My bones had shone.
                I had had rapture on my side.

from TROUBLE IN MIND

Self-Deliverance by Lion

To maul is to make a massive loss
Of the history of a body's history.

What will be taken will be the custody
Of soft tissue, and astonishment.

Her hair was a long damp chestnut
River-pelt spilled after an enormous

And important rain. Her body was still sticky
With the lilac repetitions in her cotton dress.

She was found face-up on a cold March morning
By the most menial and tender of the keepers

At the zoo, crewelled with frost marks, cursive
As the dewclaws on a lion's forepaw, massive

And significant. I had hoped for, all that Serengeti
Year, a hopelessness of less despair

Than hope itself. I knew the excellent repair
Of night fell cruel and quickly where

The lions had the mastery of me—aware
Their mastery was by my will, and fair.

Notes and Indexes

A Hunger

According to Herodotus, the ancient Egyptians believed that, after death, the human soul had to pass through various forms of incarnation for a period of 3,000 years. Plato, in *The Phaedrus,* set the period at 10,000 years (which the Philosophic Soul could reduce to a mere 3,000-year period). In *The Republic,* however, he calculates that the departed souls had to spend 1,000 years before returning to this world. In **Domestic Mysticism**, the formula of exile is derived from Empedocles, who reckoned the period of the soul's transmigration as "thrice ten-thousand seasons," or 2,500 years.

The child in **Birdie Africa**, Oyewolffe Momar Puim, was born in 1971 in Germantown, Pennsylvania. At the age of two, his mother took him from his father to join the MOVE cult in Philadelphia. All the disciples, headed by John Africa (Vincent Leaphart), changed their surnames to Africa; the child was called Birdie. In May of 1985 the police firebombed their tenement. Birdie was one of only two known to have survived the fire.

In **Real Life**, the "thirty-six things" refers to the French text, *The Thirty-Six Dramatic Situations,* written by Georges Polti in 1921, translated by Lucille Ray and published in 1977 by The Writer, Inc., Boston. According to Polti's theory, all tragic situations are based on 36 basic plots, and his analysis reduces the basis of all literature into such categories as "Fatal Imprudence" (17), "Daring Enterprise" (9), "Abduction" (16), "Obtaining" (12), "Obstacles to Love" (28), "Self-Sacrificing for an Ideal" (20).

The Future as a Cow is based on an interview with Manute Bol, the 7'7" Sudanese basketball star who, in 1985, was the starting center for the University of Bridgeport basketball team. In "Sudan to Bridgeport: The Long Journey of Manute Bol," by David H. Van Biema *(People),* Bol said: "My father was a farmer. Not a big farmer. He made some money. He sold potatoes and tomatoes. He had about 150 cows ... When I want to get married to some girl, and her father says, 'I want 100 cows,' what are you going to do if you don't have the cows? That's why you keep cows. I took care of the cows. I looked for animals that would like to kill the cows. Lions, hyenas. Sometimes I talk out loud to keep them away ... Right now I play ball. I can stay here in this country and I don't have to sell my cows, because I like the cows like my father liked them. I'm going to school right now. I play now. I can't say the future is not a cow. The cow may be my future. I don't know."

Edward VI, the speaker in **Edward VI on the Seventh Day**, was the only son born to Henry VIII. He succeeded his father as King of England and Ireland at the age of nine. He died of consumption six years later in 1553.

In the early morning hours of Wednesday, October 14, 1987, Jessica McClure, of **Jessica, from the Well**, removed a flower pot which covered a hole in her aunt's backyard in Midland, Texas. The eighteen-month-old girl slipped down through an 8-inch-wide opening into an abandoned well shaft. She remained there until her rescue on Friday evening, fifty-eight hours later. Upon her emergence from the well, psychiatrists assured the American public through the media that Jessica, though physically battered from her ordeal, would have no psychological scarring, no memory of the event.

Hitchcock Blue is based on an article which describes a blue dinner party hosted by Alfred Hitchcock. Everything in the meal was tinted blue—blue steak, blue mashed potatoes, blue utensils, blue salad, blueberries. His guests were reported to have had no comment regarding the color of the meal; dining commenced as usual.

In **The Beginning of the Beginning**, the line *I am afraid of what the world will do* is quoted from Thomas James' *Letter to a Stranger* (Houghton Mifflin, Boston, 1972).

The speaker in **Elective Mutes**, June Gibbons, is one of a set of identical twins born in 1963 at Steam Point, an RAF hospital in Aden. Beginning in their early childhood, she and her twin, Jennifer, refused to communicate with any adult; they became electively mute. As the sisters grew up together, they became more and more detached from the real world, eventually living and speaking in an invented world of poems, novels, and diaries based on the lives and rituals of their dolls. Eventually, their fantasies and languages became more symbiotic and more pathological. As they became impossibly and progressively intertwined and encoded, they began to turn on one another; they became arsonists, and eventually, they began to think of murdering one another. Now in their twenties, they are imprisoned in Broadmoor hospital for the criminally insane. All italics in the poem are quoted from the journals of June Gibbons, published in *The Silent Twins* by Marjorie Wallace (Prentice Hall Press, Englewood Cliffs, New Jersey, 1986).

In **I Wish You Love**, the references to Josef pertain to the discovery and exhumation of a grave in Embu, Brazil, on June 6, 1985. An international team of forensic scientists in São Paulo announced that the skeleton, buried under the name of Wolfgang Gerhard, was actually that of the notorious Nazi fanatic, Dr. Josef Mengele. All italics in the poem are quoted from the Charles Trenet song "Que Reste-t-il de Nos Amours." The piece was published in 1946 and was later recorded in English by Marlene Dietrich under the title "I Wish You Love."

The title **Ten Years Apprenticeship in Fantasy** refers to John Keats' request to be given a decade in which to indulge himself, watching the world before writing it all down. The epigraph for the poem, taken from "Sleep and Poetry," is as follows: *O for ten years, that I may overwhelm / Myself in poesy; so I may do the deed / That my own soul has to itself decreed.*

The title **And So Long, I've Had You Fame** was taken from the last published interview with Marilyn Monroe. She said: "Fame will go by, and, so long, I've had you fame. If it goes by, I've always known it was fickle. So at least it's something I've experienced, but that's not where I live." The interview, written by Richard Meryman, appeared in *Life* in 1962. *Cursum Perficio* ("I am finishing my journey") was etched in a tile placed outside the front door of Monroe's home in Brentwood, California.

After the Grand Perhaps was inspired by these alleged final words of François Rabelais: "I am going to seek a grand perhaps; draw the curtain, the farce is played."

The Master Letters

In the poems, many of the italicized passages without notation are from *The Letters of Emily Dickinson*. Edited by Thomas H. Johnson. Cambridge: The Belknap Press of Harvard University Press, 1958.

In the following notes, when I indicate a source, it does not necessarily mean that the quotation is verbatim. In the notes, as in the poems, archaic or anomalous spellings are intended. I use the term *refract* to mean—a nod, a pilfering—an homage, in each case, to the Original.

Carrowmore is a megalithic cemetery outside Sligo, Ireland. Many of the neglected monuments, some dating back to 4000 BC, have been partially destroyed, but three well-preserved dolmens & a rough stone circle still remain. The cremated remains of the land's original inhabitants are buried there, marked by the circumference of the stones.

Also, None Among Us Has Seen God is a line from the poem *Epistle to Be Left in the Earth* by Archibald MacLeish *(New Found Land, 1930)*.

A Rome Beauty is the name of one of the more than 10,000 varieties of chance seedling winter apples. *Heaven paints its wild irregularity* is a line from "November" of *The Shepherd's Calendar* by John Clare.

Unholy draws upon the text *The 36 Dramatic Situations* by Georges Polti, which reduces all possible dramaturgy to thirty-six possible situations. In response to an even more stringent theory which further diminishes all mortal possibilities down to a mere dozen things, I halved again that figure & came up with Six.

The term *Sentimentia,* a State of Being invented by Liam Rector, is that odd cross between dementia & sentimentality.

The final stanzas of the poem are based on the last scene in August Strindberg's *Miss Julie*.

A Brief History of Asylum was, in part, inspired by Jonathan Miller's documentary *On Madness*. Part of this film documents the fates of those incarcerated in one of America's first public asylums in the Commonwealth of Virginia. The film also recounts the history of the practice of lobotomy at the beginning of the twentieth century as a cure for schizophrenia.

The three italicized lines are quoted from the poem *Runagate, Runagate* by Robert E. Hayden.

The Supernatural Is Only the Natural, Disclosed is taken from a letter from Emily Dickinson to Thomas Wentworth Higginson, February 1863.

In **Obsession, Compulsion**, line one is an adaptation from a letter from ED to Higginson, dated 7 June 1862—*My dying Tutor told me that he would like to live till I had been a poet, but Death was much of Mob as I could master—then...*

In **Carnivorous**, the first line of the poem alludes to Anne Bradstreet's confession, upon arrival in her New World, that she was "sitting loose from God."

In **To a Strange Fashion of Forsaking**, stanza one closes with a line spoken by the angel perched atop the city of Berlin at the opening of Wim

Wender's 1988 film *Wings of Desire*—"Als ein kind ein kind war fragt er: Warum bin ich ich, und nicht du." Roughly: *When a child was a child himself, he asked himself: Why am I I, and not You?*

At the poem's center, a phrase is quoted from a letter written by Gerard Manley Hopkins to his sister Katie, 25 April 1871. And from Wyatt: *Though I myself be bridled of my mind*—And, at the close: *Schadenfreude*—a lyrical German word for a pleasure in another's woe.

For Kenneth Lincoln.

Did Not Come Back was occasioned by this passage from Viktor Frankl's Holocaust memoir *Man's Search for Meaning* (translated by Ilse Lasch):

> ... *There was a sort of self-selecting process going on the whole time among all of the prisoners. On the average, only those prisoners could keep alive who, after years of trekking from camp to camp, had lost all scruples in their fight for existence ... We who have come back, by the aid of many lucky chances or miracles—whatever one may choose to call them—we know: the best of us did not return.*

The title **And You Know That I Know Milord That You Know** is adapted from Michelangelo's sonnet 45, translated by Joseph Tusiani.

The poem is an adaptation of this parable: the proverbial hermit searches in the darkness for the light, while all along carrying a bright lantern in his own right hand. In this instance, I've inverted the image—the monk has been living, unbeknownst to himself, in the light all the while, clasping a lantern of dark.

The October Horse is a figure from an ancient autumnal harvest sacrificial ritual described in James G. Frazer's *The Golden Bough*.

The line *I had a yearning I could tell to none* is a refracted version of these lines from a letter from ED to Higginson, dated 25 April 1862—*I had a terror—since September—I could tell to none—and so I sing, as the Boy does by the Burying Ground—because I am afraid—*

In **Gratitude**, halcion is the name of the benzodiazepine hypnotic agent banned in America in the early 1990s. Like the kingfisher (halcyon-bird), which has the power to calm the wind & sea during the winter solstice while it nested, it had the power to compose.

Dull Weather is homage to the Boys of Autumn, who, each October, *grow suicidally beautiful... And gallop terribly against each other's bodies* (James Wright).

The close of the poem alludes to a prediction in "The [Old] Farmer's

Almanack, Calculated on a New & Improved Plan, for the Year of Our Lord, 1857" by Robert B. Thomas.

The nobody in **Radiating Naïveté** was occasioned by William Blake's notion of his false god "Nobodaddy."

Fair Copy from a Fair World was occasioned, in part, by the work of Primo Levi. And from the work of Thomas James' *Letters to A Stranger* (he used the image more than once): ... *a ceremony / That wishes to marry an absence.*

His Apprentice makes loose & various reference to Dr. Faustus, first mentioned in a letter dated 20 August 1507. It is known that a certain Georgius Sabellius, calling himself Faust Junin, obtained toward the end of Lent the position of schoolmaster at Kreuznach, Germany. He was soon thereafter dismissed from his position because of his compulsion to punish randomly his young wards.

In **You Can't Always Get What You Want**, the line—*All boys should be nicer* is refracted from Richard Hugo's "The Lady in Kicking Horse Reservoir."

The opening of **Pursuit of Happiness** is taken from a letter from William Blake to John Trusler, 23 August 1799.

The phrase **A Glooming Peace This Morning with It Brings** is taken from the Prince's speech in the last act, final scene of *Romeo & Juliet*.

Haute Couture Vulgarity was inspired by these two articles, first—an omnibus review in the *Washington Post Book World*, Christmas Day 1988, which begins: *Lucie Brock-Broido is the poet laureate of* People *magazine ... &* continues: *Nothing inhuman is alien to her ... [She] so overestimates an interest in haute couture vulgarity ...* The second was a piece in *People* magazine entitled *Turned Off By TV, Soft Music & Sweets, Four Nuns Rebel, Aiming to Keep the Cloister Their Oyster.*
  Italics in stanza four are homage to Robert Creeley's *I Know A Man*.

The term **Toxic Gumbo** was coined by Amos Favorite, a retired aluminum plant worker, president of a fledgling environmentalist organization called *Ascension Parish Residents Against Toxic Pollution*. Favorite said, of his corridor in Louisiana, that he & his neighbors were living in a "toxic gumbo" of vinyl chloride, benzene, mercury, chloroform, & other chemicals stewing the air. Here, the gumbos refer to certain antidepressant medications.

In the Attitude Desired for Exhibition is about the art of taxidermy. The slack skin of the animal must be poised & wired in the attitude or pose that the taxidermist deems appropriate for exhibition.

Lissadell, the once stately now decaying home of Sir Henry Gore-Booth, is a classical mansion near Drumcliffe in Ireland.

Also, homage & refract in the poem to G.M. Hopkins' sonnet, *Carrion Comfort*.

Like Murder for Small Hay in the Underworld is my own mis-reading of a handwritten facsimile of Robert Frost's *Tribute to E.A. Robinson*—"I was tried without feeling or sentiment like murder for small pay in the underworld."

In Native American hunting ritual, it is considered necessary, when one slaughters an animal, to feed & to offer water to the carcass so that its spirit can pass on to the next world.

The title **Everybody Has a Heart, Except Some People** is a line spoken by Margo Channing, played by Bette Davis in the 1950 Joseph L. Mankiewicz film, *All About Eve*.

The title **Moving On in the Dark Like Loaded Boats at Night, Though There Is No Course, There Is Boundlessness** is from a letter written by ED to Susan Gilbert Dickinson. Line one is, in part, based on ED's letter to Higginson, June 1869. In this letter, written after her third refusal to travel to Boston, Dickinson has invited Higginson to Amherst, explaining that she is Home-bound:

> You noticed my dwelling alone—To an Emigrant, Country is idle except it be his own. You speak kindly of seeing me. Could it please your convenience to come so far as Amherst I should be very glad, but I do not cross my Father's ground to any House or town.

Your Cromwell, Your Thomas More makes reference to Henry VIII's monarchical dependence on his inner circle of advisors, his flock, all male. Sir Thomas More, eventually deemed treasonous & heretical by Henry, was beheaded on Tower Hill on 6 July 1535.

The poem closes with the valediction of a letter from Henry to Anne Boleyn, composed during their courtship, & dated September 1528:

> No more to yow at thys present, myne own darlyng, for lake off tyme, but that I wolde you were in myne arms or I in yours, for I thynk it long syns I kyst you … By the hand off hym whyche I trust shortly shallbe yours, Henry R.

The title **I Dont Know Who It Is, That Sings, nor Did I, Would I Tell** is from a letter from ED to her uncle, Joseph A. Sweetser, Amherst, July 1858.

For Ravi Desai.

A **Grimoire** is a manual of black magic used to cast spells, invoke demons, et cetera. Ichor is the ethereal fluid which flows through the veins of the gods.

In **Work**, *I hid me*—is taken from John Clare's *A Vision*.

The term "terrible crystals" is adapted from a letter to Gerard Manley Hopkins, dated 26 October 1881, from Richard Watson Dixon. Dixon wrote, in response to work sent to him by Hopkins: *I can understand that your present position, seclusion and exercises would give to your writings a rare charm— they have done so in those that I have seen: something that I cannot describe, but know to myself by the inadequate word* terrible pathos—*something of what you call temper in poetry: a right temper which goes to the point of the terrible; the terrible crystal.*

The Last Passenger Pigeon in the Cincinnati Zoo is based upon the extinction of the passenger pigeon in North America. After the turn of the nineteenth century, though these birds had formerly numbered in the billions, by the spring of 1914, the last of this species, a female in captivity, expired.

The italics in the poem are from a letter to Richard Woodhouse from John Keats, dated 27 October 1818:

> *I feel assured I should write from the mere yearning and fondness I have for the Beautiful even if my night's labours should be burnt every morning and no eye ever shine on them.*

In **Everything Husk to the Will**, several lines are based on the anonymous early Anglo-Saxon poem, *The Ruin*, translated by Michael Alexander.

The line *If it darken if a shadow* is from the Emily Brontë poem dated 12 July 1836. That poem, written in a child's incantatory voice, tells how the course of a day's hours, its weather—should be taken as prediction of a girl's destiny.

For my first father, David Simon Broido (1924–1968).

In **The Interrupted Life**, the italicized lines are adapted from Ezra Pound's translation of Li-Po/Rihaku's poem *The River-Merchant's Wife*. The title is taken from the name of an exhibition in Soho on the bounty & relentlessness & postures of Deaths.

How Can It Be I Am No Longer I is based, in part, on the deaths of conjoined twins who were connected at the sternum & shared a three-chambered heart—a condition which prevented surgeons from separating them at birth. Though they were not expected to live past even a year, they survived till the age of seven. On the evening of 22 July 1991, they died within the hour of each other.

The title is taken from the opening line of an untitled madrigal by Michelangelo, circa 1511.

The Sleeping Hollow of His Face Will Be the Straight Pass of Surrendering is for my father, Joel Greenwald (1920–1986).

Am Moor was provoked by the work of Georg Trakl. The German title of his poem, *Am Moor*, has been translated as "On the Marshy Pastures," or, more simply, "On the Moors." In August of 1914, Trakl served as a lieutenant-pharmacist in the Austrian army. After the battle of Grodek, he was left in a barn with ninety wounded men in his charge. Suffering great depression from his work, he was assigned, several months thereafter, to a hospital—not as a corpsman, but as a patient. In November, he died of an overdose of his own pharmaceuticals in Krakow, Poland.

—*& with gratitude for those who have watched over these*—

Frank Bidart, Sophie Cabot Black, Ed Brunner, Timothy Donnelly, Kenneth Lincoln, Stephen McLeod, Liam Rector, Sue Standing, Tree Swenson. And to Helen Vendler. And to Harry Ford.

Trouble in Mind

In a small notebook called "Pieces of Paper," Wallace Stevens transcribed several hundred titles for poems which he never wrote. From this journal, I've adapted the following: "The Halo That Would Not Light," "Still Life with Aspirin," "The One Theme of Which Everything Else Is a Variation," "Basic Poem in a Basic Tongue," "Morgue Near Heaven," "Darwinism as Spite" (from "Communism as Spite"), and "The Identity of the Bridegroom."

Stevens's notebook is reproduced in George S. Lensing's *Wallace Stevens: A Poet's Growth* (Baton Rouge and London: Louisiana State University Press, 1986).

In **Still Life with Aspirin**, the line *For a poem to be true, it must "come from an Ever"* has as its source the following transcription from Stevens's notebook:

> Qualities of a poem
>   interesting
>   indigenous to a person
>   d'un daemon
>   felt words
>   capable of infuriating
>   with
>   poetry emotion
>   to come from an ever
>   free source
>   esser [sic]: [essor (Fr.); swarm or group flight]
>   effortless
>   contagious

Some of the language in **Leaflet on Wooing** is drawn from the Seventh of Rilke's *Duino Elegies*. In the Stephen Mitchell translation, the poem begins: *Not wooing, no longer shall wooing, voice that has outgrown it, / be the nature of your cry*.

The title **Death as a German Expert** is adapted from a line in John Berryman's "Dream Song No. 41."

The phrase **Soul Keeping Company** refers to an ancient Jewish mourning ritual. According to tradition, even after death, the soul stays hovering until the body itself is properly buried. The body cannot be left alone for even an hour, and guardians must keep constant vigil, affording company for the soul during its most difficult time.

Kaspar Hauser was the name given to the child who, on Whit-Monday 1828, mysteriously appeared in the town square of Nuremberg. He was feral and had no speech save one sentence: "I would like to be a horseman like my father." He would take only bread and water. Eventually, the boy became the ward of Ritter Anselm von Feuerbach until, in 1833, Kaspar was attacked and stabbed to death by an unknown assailant.

The close of **Girl at the Border of Her Own Allegory** is based on Jean Cocteau's 1946 film, *La Belle et la Bête*. At the Beast's High Gothic castle, he keeps a white stallion with a tinseled mane. The horse, Magnificat, can transport its rider to any imagined destination without instruction or direction.

The opening image in **The One Thousand Days** refers to the Japanese custom of placing a dish of salt outside the front door of the home where a family member has recently died.

The largest known species of wolf, the **Dire Wolf**, roamed the North American continent until its extinction during the Pleistocene period.

The title **Self-Deliverance by Lion** is adapted from Kay Redfield Jamison's *Night Falls Fast*. In 1995, the body of a thirty-six-year-old transient woman from Little Rock was discovered by a worker at the National Zoo in Washington. She had scaled a barrier, ascended a rough high wall, and crossed a twenty-six-foot moat in order to make her way into the lions' den. Her death by mauling was ruled a suicide.

From Daniel 6:24, I've adapted the following: *The lions had the mastery of them /And broke all their bones in pieces.*

Index of Titles

After Raphael	102
After the Grand Perhaps	43
Also, None Among Us Has Seen God	52
Am Moor	97
And So Long, I've Had You Fame	42
And You Know That I Know Milord That You Know	62
Autobiography	10
Basic Poem in a Basic Tongue	110
The Beginning of the Beginning	28
Birdie Africa	5
Boy at the Border of His Own Allegory	116
A Brief History of Asylum	55
Carnivorous	59
Carrowmore	51
Danse Macabre	26
Darwinism as Spite	121
Death as a German Expert	111
The Deerhunting	120
Did Not Come Back	61
Dire Wolf	138
Domestic Mysticism	3
Dull Weather	66
Edward VI on the Seventh Day	14
Elective Mutes	33
Everybody Has a Heart, Except Some People	82
Everything Husk to the Will	90
Evolution	8
Fair Copy from a Fair World	71
Fragment on Dissembling	122
From the Proscenium	67
The Future as a Cow	13
Gamine	112

Girl at the Border of Her Own Allegory	126
A Glooming Peace This Morning with It Brings	75
Gratitude	65
Grimoire	86
The Halo That Lit Twice	123
The Halo That Would Not Light	101
Haute Couture Vulgarity	77
Heartbeat	25
Herculaneum	106
His Apprentice	72
Hitchcock Blue	22
Housekeeping	76
How Can It Be I Am No Longer I	94
I Dont Know Who It Is, That Sings, nor Did I, Would I Tell	85
I Wish You Love	38
The Identity of the Bridegroom	132
In a Landlocked Time	29
In Elsinore	128
In the Attitude Desired for Exhibition	80
The Insignificants	114
The Interrupted Life	93
Jessica, from the Well	17
Kid Flash	23
Lady with an Ermine	122
The Last Passenger Pigeon in the Cincinnati Zoo	89
Leaflet on Wooing	103
Like Murder for Small Hay in the Underworld	81
A Lion in Winter	115
Lucie & Her Sisters	31
Morgue Near Heaven	113
Moving On in the Dark Like Loaded Boats at Night…	83
Obsession, Compulsion	58
The October Horse	63
October Seventh, Nineteen Eighty-Three	11
Of the Finished World	127

The One Theme of Which Everything Else Is a Variation	107
The One Thousand Days	136
Pamphlet on Ravening	139
Periodic Table of Ethereal Elements	108
Physicism	134
Portrait of Lucy with Fine Nile Jar	130
A Preamble *to The Master Letters*	49
Pursuit of Happiness	74
Radiating Naïveté	69
Real Life	9
Rome Beauty	53
Self-Deliverance by Lion	140
Self-Portrait as a Herd of One	133
Self-Portrait as Kaspar Hauser	124
Self-Portrait with Her Hair Cut Off	135
Self-Portrait with Her Hair on Fire	119
Self-Portrait with Self-Pity	125
The Sleeping Hollow of His Face…	96
Some Details of Hell	109
Soul Keeping Company	118
Spain	129
Still Life with Aspirin	104
Still Life with Feral Horse	117
The Supernatural Is Only the Natural, Disclosed	57
Ten Years Apprenticeship in Fantasy	40
To a Strange Fashion of Forsaking	60
Toxic Gumbo	79
Unholy	54
What the Whales Sound Like in Manhattan	27
Work	87
You Can't Always Get What You Want	73
Your Cromwell, Your Thomas More	84

Index of First Lines

A boy phones from a Frankish-	116
A man takes off his armor past the Iron Age	126
After the Zhivago of it all, the terrible sleeve	76
After vespers, after the first snow	43
All about Carrowmore the lambs	51
Am I to be a patient	79
Am lean against	97
An annulment of a species is as keen	89
And twenty-four wild Novembers, two	90
As long as the lions are rampant, I will stay	115
At dawn they are beginning	28
At Lissadell I am the red she	80
At your feet, I am a shoemaker's apprentice	57
Born in the dark, you come back up	23
Curious in your dark	122
Dear Master—	54
Dear One—	81
Father is a large man	14
From the great warm side of the animal	13
Heart, be clean. Fists, be open, numb	112
Here is the maudlin petty bourgeoisie of ruin	110
How odd that she would die into an August	42
I am a false philosopher of this	69
I am alive, this morning—	65
I was lying loose from God. Strange is it not best	59
I was not ready for your form to be cold	108
If I imagine him healthy in his distressed	113
In ruthless October, the salt flats dry out	84
In summertime, when we were little, I remember we	33
In the principalities	125
In the roan hour between then & then again…	61
In the snow, white noise, a gathering	122

In the tameless night season	86
In the valley of the Euphrates, each	134
In thrice 10,000 seasons, I will come back to this world	3
Innocence is a catarrh of the mind, distressed	107
It is love and its relinquish	117
It is only three o'clock & already I'm alone	10
It is time now to turn off the devices in the wing	109
It's not enough to have my one dream in hand…	31
Let me be brief then	25
Like Josef's skull ascending from Brazilian soil	38
Like the Shropshire clock with its pocked off-white face	135
Lord, one day you'll find these in a locked box, unlocked	87
Master— ('I Don't Know Who It Is, That Sings…')	85
Master— ('To a Stange Fashion of Forsaking')	60
Master, my tinsmith—	71
Master, then This—I crossed my father's gate	83
My Apparition—Lord	93
My Darling C,	40
My Dear Sir—	67
My father calls me Wolf	5
My innocence diminishes in the thrall	55
My Most Courteous Lord—	52
My mother says in the beautiful	53
My torso is a cedar chest in the brief closet	130
No one is bored, just barbaric	106
Now, it is as dark as the pathos of pushing a wheel-	119
One day he wakened from	96
One night you will walk into a flume	132
Open the final book: November spills	127
Perhaps it isn't possible to say these things	102
Revd Sir—	74
Rises, sets, by my own hand, dog days end	66
Shepherd—Fasten him to the hearth	63
Sir	73
Soon the electrical wires will grow heavy under the snow	9

Sorrows, like a gathering of dire wolves, come in packs. …	138
Tell me the story now in such	114
Tell me where in what penultimate white	123
That I had no idea I had been travelling	62
The Breath is as much of Mob as I can master, love. Steamy	58
The extinct creatures would have liked this day	8
The god-leash leaves	129
The heart is a place made slippery	121
The hours between washing and the well	118
The North Star hanging	111
The reason why I love the orchard is my propensity for lavish	133
The sedative of frost composes	75
There had been some small confusion, some	27
There is nothing like the mistral lull	29
There is the mourning dish of salt	136
There she was, the mother of me, like a lit plinth	104
There would be a boy	128
These we take for granted	22
This is what it was like: the morning	17
To maul is to make a massive loss	140
To Recipient Unknown—	77
Wanting is reposed and plump	103
We were preparing to miss our President and his	120
What the sailors thought on that last night	26
What was it like then?	124
When everything seems a message	11
When, after many years, the raptor beak	101
Winter was the ravaging in the scarified	94
You cannot will intoxication, vertigo, a ravening or wild	139
You did not state your price. When you took	72
You have fed me on Air too long—a daguerreotype	82